Norway

Norway

BY WIL MARA

Enchantment of the World™
Second Series

CHILDREN'S PRESS®

An Imprint of Scholastic Inc.

Frontispiece: **Bergen**

Consultant: Christine Ingebritsen, PhD, Professor of Scandinavian Studies, University of Washington, Seattle, Washington
Please note: All statistics are as up-to-date as possible at the time of publication.

Book production by The Design Lab

Library of Congress Cataloging-in-Publication Data
Names: Mara, Wil, author.
Title: Norway / by Wil Mara.
Description: New York : Children's Press, [2017] | Series: Enchantment of the
    world | Includes bibliographical references and index.
Identifiers: LCCN 2016025112 | ISBN 9780531220917 (library binding)
Subjects: LCSH: Norway—Juvenile literature.
Classification: LCC DL409 .M37 2017 | DDC 948.1—dc23
LC record available at https://lccn.loc.gov/2016025112

1 2 3 4 5 6 7 8 9 10 R 26 25 24 23 22 21 20 19 18 17

Lofoten Islands

Contents

Left to right: **At a fjord, mountains, polar bear, northern lights, Viking carving**

CHAPTER 1

The Comfort of Home

JONAS AND HIS LITTLE SISTER SIGRID ARE SITTING IN Jonas's bedroom, playing a trivia game on her tablet. The device was a gift for her last birthday, and Jonas has one, too. They also have their own phones, flat-screen TVs, and laptops. Their house is three stories high, with a big backyard and a swimming pool. Their mother and father both drive new cars. Both Jonas and Sigrid get weekly allowances. They're supposed to do work around the house to earn it, but their parents don't make them stick to this rule all the time.

Jonas and Sigrid know they're lucky. Some of their friends don't have all the nice things they do. They don't think any less of these friends because their parents aren't as rich. They have been taught that everyone is equal, that money isn't everything, and that you should never think you're superior just because you have more than someone else.

Opposite: **The average Norwegian family includes two children.**

Jonas and Ingrid's mother and father both have jobs. Their mother is a bookkeeper for an accounting firm, and their father is an oil company executive. He has worked in the oil industry for a long time. He wears a suit and tie on most days and carries a briefcase. Sometimes he has to travel for his company. Every now and then he'll take his family with him. Jonas and Ingrid

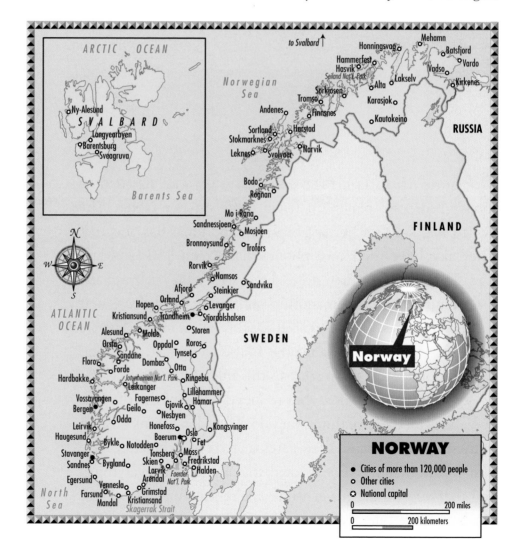

have loved these trips. They've been to Russia, Spain, Italy, England, and the United States. Sigrid has a particular love for traveling and thinks she might want to work in the airline industry one day. Maybe she'll be a pilot. Who knows?

A mother and child look down at Lysefjord, one of the more than one thousand fjords that mark the Norwegian coastline.

Life in the North

Jonas and Sigrid live in Norway, one of the most northerly countries in Europe. Much of Norway's landscape is rough, rugged, and rocky. The nation is renowned for its dramatic sea inlets bounded by towering mountains. These are called fjords (fee-ORDZ). Norway also has thousands of glaciers, moving masses of ice formed over the years as snow builds up and compresses into ice.

Workers on a drilling platform in the North Sea. More than two hundred thousand people work in Norway's oil and gas industry.

Norway's economy is one of the healthiest in the world. Oil was discovered beneath the ocean floor in Norwegian territory in the 1960s. Wealth from this oil has enabled the Norwegian government to provide well for its people. It pays for most health care and education. People are given many months off from work when their children are young, and generous pensions when they themselves are old. The standard of living is high and so is the cost of living. Norway is now one of the most expensive countries in the world.

An Equal Society

Norway has a strong commitment to equality. Norwegians believe that everyone should be treated equally, regardless of their race, gender, age, religion, education, or wealth. Government benefits help smooth out inequality in wealth.

And so do the attitudes of the people. Most Norwegians dislike it when people display too much pride or arrogance. So a doctor and a clerk, for example, chat easily as equals, calling each other by their first names.

Norwegians work hard, but they are committed to prioritizing time with their families. They seldom stay late at work, and they look forward to time off. Many Norwegians have a country house, a small cabin where they can escape the city. They go to hike, sail, and enjoy the beautiful land. But mostly, they just want to relax, enjoying the warm coziness of time with their family.

During winter in Norway there is a lot of snow to play in.

CHAPTER 2

Dramatic Land

NORWAY IS ONE OF THE MOST NORTHERLY COUNTRIES in Europe. It is part of a region called the Scandinavian Peninsula, which includes Sweden and sections of Finland and Russia.

Although Norway is similar in area to the U.S. state of Montana, it is relatively long and narrow. It borders Sweden, Finland, Russia, and three large bodies of water—the Barents Sea to the north, the Norwegian Sea to the west, and the North Sea to the south. A smaller body of water, the Skagerrak Strait, is between southern Norway, Sweden, and Denmark.

Opposite: **Hikers in Norway take a footpath to Jostedal Glacier, the largest glacier in mainland Europe.**

Norway's Geographic Features

Area: 125,021 square miles (323,802 sq km)

Highest Elevation: Galdhopiggen, 8,100 feet (2,469 m) above sea level

Lowest Elevation: Sea level along the coast

Longest River: Glomma River, 372 miles (599 km) long

Largest Lake: Mjosa, 142 square miles (368 sq km)

Longest Fjord: Sognefjord, 127 miles (204 km)

Warmest Month: July, with an average daytime temperature of 71°F (22°C)

Coolest Month: January, with an average daytime temperature of 31°F (–0.5°C)

Average Annual Precipitation: In Oslo, 30 inches (76 cm)

Highest Recorded Temperature: 96.1°F (35.6°C) in Nesbyen, Buskerud, June 1970

Lowest Recorded Temperature: –60.5°F (–51.4°C) in Karasjok, Finnmark, January 1886

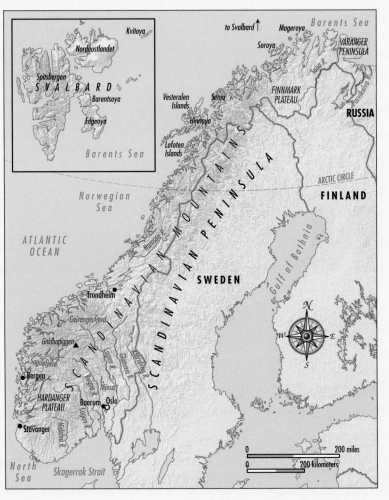

Much of Norway lies above the Arctic Circle, an imaginary circle around the earth at about 66° North latitude. This circle represents the latitude north of which the sun never sets for at least twenty-four hours in a row once a year. Similarly, for at least one day in the winter, the sun never rises.

Land of the Midnight Sun

Norway is sometimes called the Land of the Midnight Sun because so much of it lies north of the Arctic Circle and experiences days when the sun never sets. Moving north from the Arctic Circle, the periods of continuous daytime and continuous nighttime get longer. For example, in Longyearbyen, a town in Svalbard, a group of Norwegian islands in the remote Arctic Ocean, the sun is above the horizon continuously for 126 days, from April 19 to August 23. The sun is below the horizon in Longyearbyen from October 26 to February 15. (The North Pole itself experiences six months of continuous daylight and six months of continuous dark.)

During periods of the midnight sun, the sun is not directly overhead. Instead, it sits low in the sky, moving around the horizon over the course of the day. During the wintertime polar night, when the sun never rises above the horizon, the land is cast in little more than a dim blue.

The midnight sun occurs because Earth is tilted on its axis in relation to the Sun. As Earth turns, the regions facing away from the Sun fall into night. But when the Northern Hemisphere is tilted toward the Sun, the extreme northern regions remain bathed in sunlight as Earth turns. When the Northern Hemisphere is tilted away from the Sun, the sunlight never hits the North Pole. These same effects happen at the southern end of the globe, but at opposite times of the year.

A cruise ship travels up Geirangerfjord. It is one of the most visited fjords in Norway, renowned for its steep walls and beautiful scenery.

Shaping Norway

Thousands of years ago, most of the land known today as Norway was covered by ice. As time passed, those massive sheets of ice moved, gouging deep scars in the land. Norway's present form began to take shape as the ice sheets moved. The movement of the glaciers created gorges, basins, and valleys. As the glaciers melted and the surrounding seas rose, these features filled with water. Today, these dramatic inlets, called fjords, define Norway's jagged coastline.

Norway is famous for its fjords. It boasts nearly 1,200 fjords, more than any other nation. Norway's fjords are admired for their astonishing beauty, with mountains rising directly from the sea. Sognefjord is the longest fjord in Norway, stretching 127 miles (204 kilometers). Geirangerfjord is considered especially beautiful, with its towering rock walls and stunning waterfalls that pour down the cliffs.

Mountains and Flatlands

Away from the jagged coast, Norway features both mountains and flatlands. The Scandinavian Mountain region runs south–north along the border with Sweden and continues into parts

A visitor stands on Trolltunga ("troll's tongue" in Norwegian), a spectacular rock ledge that juts out above Lake Ringedalsvatnet in southwestern Norway.

Norway is filled with majestic mountain peaks.

of western Finland. It is around 1,100 miles (1,800 km) long and 200 miles (322 km) wide in some areas. The mountains are rugged and steep, with many sheer cliffs. The highest point in the country is a mountain peak called Galdhopiggen, which towers 8,100 feet (2,469 meters) above sea level. Located in the southern Scandinavian Mountains, it is the highest point in all of Scandinavia.

The southern part of the nation tends to be a bit less mountainous than the northern part, but is still hilly. Forest abounds, the climate is milder, and in some places the soil is fertile enough for agriculture.

Norway also features broad plains and plateaus. In southeastern Norway is the Hardanger Plateau, a flat, almost featureless region cut by many rivers. In the extreme north of Norway, a region called Finnmark is the nation's largest plateau. Few people live on the Finnmark Plateau, a cold, rugged region marked by lakes and bogs.

Norway's landscape is dominated by lakes. It has sixty-five thousand of them. The largest is Mjosa, a long, skinny lake north of Oslo. Norway also has many rivers. The Glomma River, the nation's longest, runs south through the southern half of Norway, before emptying into the Skagerrak Strait at Fredrikstad.

A reindeer stands out against the fall colors of the tundra in northern Norway.

Mountains rise abruptly from the sea in the Lofoten Islands.

Many Islands

Tens of thousands of islands are scattered along Norway's broken coastline. The largest, including Hinnoya and Senja, lie in the north. The Lofoten Islands in northern Norway were once the center of Norway's vibrant cod fishing industry.

Norway also claims an archipelago—a cluster of islands—in the Arctic Ocean, about halfway between the northern tip of Norway and the North Pole. Called Svalbard, several of these islands are even larger than the islands near the coast. Svalbard first fell under Norway's jurisdiction in 1920,

A Look at Norway's Cities

Norway's largest city is its capital, Oslo, which was home to 660,987 people in 2016. Bergen (below) is Norway's second-largest city, with a population of about 280,000. The city, which sits on a peninsula in southwestern Norway, was founded in the late 1000s and became a busy trading port. Today, Bergen remains a busy commercial area, serving the shipping and oil industries. It also has some of the mildest winters in the nation.

Trondheim, Norway's third-largest city with a population of about 188,000, lies in central Norway at the mouth of the Nidelva River. Like Bergen, it is mostly surrounded by water. Trondheim began as a trading post in the late 900s and was an important site for sailors. It was also a center of Catholic activity. Nidaros Cathedral, built in 1070, drew pilgrims from throughout Scandinavia. When Protestantism came to Norway

in the 1500s, Nidaros Cathedral became a Lutheran church. Today, Trondheim is a center of science, technology, and medicine.

Norway's fourth-largest city is Stavanger (above), which has a population of about 133,000. Located in the southwestern part of the nation, it too sits on a peninsula. Stavanger was founded in the early 1100s, and by the 1700s it had grown into a bustling commercial area. Many of the houses from that period are still standing and are protected by law. In more recent times, Stavanger grew following the boom provided by the discovery of oil in the North Sea. Today, the city's unemployment rate is lower than it is in most of the nation. Shipping and shipbuilding are major industries there.

Dramatic Land **23**

although whalers and other sailors had been using the islands since the 1600s. The islands are an important spot for migrating birds, as they have a relatively mild climate for such a northern locale. Only about three thousand people live on Svalbard, so the birds are generally undisturbed.

The Climate

In much of Norway, there is snow on the ground for more than one hundred days every year.

Norway lies as far north as Alaska, so some people assume that it is always cold. But unlike Alaska, Norway's climate is warmed by an ocean current called the Gulf Stream, which

Dancing Lights

Norway is one of the best places in the world to see the aurora borealis, or northern lights. This spectacular light show occurs when charged particles from the sun collide with gases in earth's upper atmosphere. The result is colorful bands of light dancing across the sky. The northern lights are most often green, but they can also be red, purple, yellow, or other colors. In Norway, the northern lights are most often seen in the northern part of the country on cold, clear winter nights.

carries warm water all the way from the Caribbean Sea to its west coast. Because of the warming effect of the Gulf Stream, Norwegian farmers can grow crops north of the Arctic Circle.

In Norway, winter begins around November and is in full swing by January. This is the coldest time of the year, with average daytime temperatures of 20 to 30 degrees Fahrenheit (−7 to −1 degree Celsius). Days are mildest along the coast and become chillier farther inland. The coldest region is the Finnmark Plateau, where winter temperatures hover around 5°F (−15°C). Upper reaches of the mountainous areas also get extremely cold. The winds tend to be stronger on mountaintops as well, making the air feel even colder.

Spring comes around mid-March and lasts until May. The heat of the sun as the days lengthen melts the snow and ice that formed over the previous months, and temperatures rise. Trees and shrubs become green again, and flowers emerge. In the south, crops begin growing. In the more northerly areas, the air is still cool. But the long and dark days of winter begin to taper off. Along the western coast, conditions are often pleasant, and people enjoy the sunshine.

People relax at Sognsvann Lake in Oslo on a warm summer day.

The Thor Heyerdahl Institute

Located in southern Norway, not far from the capital city of Oslo, is the town of Larvik. It is the birthplace of Norwegian adventurer Thor Heyerdahl. Born in 1914, Heyerdahl showed an early interest in the sciences, particularly animal biology. He then became interested in geography, which sparked an urge toward world travel. In 1947, he and a group of friends built a raft out of wood and sailed from Peru across the Pacific to the Tuamotu Islands. They had named the raft the *Kon-Tiki*, and Heyerdahl wrote a book about the journey called *The Kon-Tiki Expedition by Raft Across the South Seas*. It became a best seller, and a movie made about the journey won the Best Documentary Feature Academy Award in 1951.

Heyerdahl continued with more adventures throughout his life, emphasizing the similarities that bind cultures rather than the differences that divide them. He died in 2002 at the age of eighty-seven. Two years earlier, an institute bearing his name had been built in his hometown of Larvik. Today, it is a center for the promotion of international dialogue and multicultural cooperation, geographical research, and environmental protection around the world.

Summer in Norway means sunny days. It is warm, but not hot, with average daytime temperatures in July around 70°F (21°C). People wear shorts and T-shirts, but even in the south, temperatures rarely rise above 80°F (27°C).

Temperatures begin to dip again in September as Norway enters another autumn. The forested regions come alive with fall colors, a period that does not last long because the temperature drops quickly. Hints of winter are felt as early as mid-October, but generally, winter doesn't really come until November.

CHAPTER 3

The Wild Side

A WHITE-TAILED EAGLE SOARS LOW OVER A FJORD, ready to snatch a fish from the water. An arctic fox curls up in its den, its thick fur keeping it warm while a howling snowstorm rages outside. A humpback whale bursts from beneath the water, twisting majestically before it descends again beneath the waves.

Norway abounds with life. It is home to about one hundred types of mammals, two hundred kinds of fish, and nearly five hundred bird species. These creatures each have their own way of dealing with the cold.

Opposite: **Fireweed grows well in northern climates such as Norway. This colorful wildflower grows up to 6 feet (2 m) tall.**

Reptiles and Amphibians

Grass snakes usually live at the edge of woods or fields. In the winter, they spend much of their time underground, protected from the cold weather.

Reptiles and amphibians are rare in Norway because they are cold-blooded. This means that their body temperatures are determined by the temperature of their environment. In the summer in Norway, reptiles can warm themselves during the long sunny days, but they cannot do that in the winter.

The largest reptile species in Norway is the giant leatherback sea turtle. Norway is also home to several species of frogs, two types of salamanders, and three species of snakes. The grass snake is one of Norway's hardiest reptile species. Widespread in Europe and west-central Asia, the grass snake typically grows about 3 feet (1 m) long. It lives mostly in watery environments, as it feeds mostly on amphibians such

To Sea and Back Again

The leatherback sea turtle is the largest of all turtle species. It grows more than 6 feet (2 m) long and can weigh 2,000 pounds (900 kilograms). Leatherbacks migrate an average of 3,700 miles (6,000 km) between their feeding areas and their breeding areas. That's farther than the distance from New York City to London, England. Leatherbacks spend most of their time feeding in the open ocean, but then they always return to the same area to breed. Some leatherbacks come back to the Norway beach year after year to lay their eggs. Hundreds sometimes come ashore in the same place in a single night in order to dig nests. The mothers lay their eggs, cover the nests, and then crawl back to the water and disappear in the waves.

as frogs. Other food items include fish and crustaceans. If a grass snake feels threatened, it may go through a dramatic routine of "playing dead," in which it turns onto its back, opens its mouth, and lets its forked tongue dangle out. This deters predators. Norway is also home to two other snake species: the common viper and the smooth snake.

Mammals

A wide variety of mammals live in Norway. They range from large land animals like wolves, bears, musk ox, arctic foxes, reindeer, and elk to smaller creatures such as rabbits, shrews, and hedgehogs. The larger land mammals are most likely to be found in forested areas, usually in the mountainous regions. Smaller animals have often become well adapted to living near

Polar bears have thick fur that helps keep them warm on land. They also have a layer of fat as much as 4.5 inches (11.5 cm) thick that preserves bodily warmth in the water.

humans and might live in cities or suburbs. Most Norwegian mammal species are carnivores, animals that eat other animals. Very few, however, are threatening to humans. One exception is the polar bear, which in Norway lives only on the Svalbard Islands. The smaller brown bears live on the mainland of Norway, but people are unlikely to encounter them.

Mammals also live in the waters off Norway. Seals and walruses move between the sea and the land, while a wide variety of species of dolphins and whales live in the water. In summer, it is not unusual to see sperm, humpback, and minke whales coming up for air along the Norwegian coast. Like all mammals, whales use lungs to breathe air. Sperm whales can hold their breath for an hour, but most whales come up for a breath about every fifteen minutes. They do this through their blowholes, which are like nostrils. In Norway, the best place to see whales is the Vesteralen Islands in the north. Many people come to this rugged land hoping to see sperm and humpback whales leaping from the water.

A humpback whale breaks through the surface of the water while feeding on herring. The humpback leaps upward through a school of herring, grabbing as many of the small fish in its gaping mouth as possible.

Whaling: Tradition and Controversy

In centuries past, mighty whales filled the world's oceans. Because of their huge size, they became prized hunting targets. Whalers wanted both their meat, which could be preserved for later use, and their large layer of fat, called blubber, which was used to make lamp oil, soap, candles, and much more. Because whales were so valuable, whaling became a huge business. Many species were already in decline by the mid-1800s, and some experts estimate that another three million whales were killed in the 1900s. Over a century, the population of some species dropped by 90 percent. By the 1980s, the situation was dire, and most countries agreed to stop whaling.

Today, Norway is one of just three countries in the world that hunt whales. (The others are Iceland and Japan.) Norwegians have been whaling since Viking times, and some Norwegians argue that it is an important cultural tradition. The only whales that Norwegians hunt today are minke whales, which are not endangered. The Norwegian government says it is important to keep Norway's whaling tradition alive, and that the whale meat is needed as food. But Norwegians eat an average of just a half a pound (0.2 kg) of whale meat

per year. In fact, much of the meat produced by the Norwegian whaling industry is sent to Japan. Some of it is also used as animal feed in Norway. Because of this, many people around the world consider the Norwegian whaling industry unnecessary and have called on Norway to end the practice.

Fish

Norway has thousands of lakes, streams, ponds, and rivers, along with an extraordinarily long coastline, so it has plenty of water where fish can live. Freshwater fishing is a popular pastime in the country, as there is abundant fish such as trout, whitefish, flounder, and char. In the sea are sizable numbers of cod, hake, and pollock.

The Atlantic salmon is one of the most common species. It is found throughout the chilly waters of the northern Atlantic Ocean, as far west as North America. Young salmon spend the first few years of their lives in the river where they were born. After a few years, when they are old enough, they venture into the sea. They return to the stream or river of their youth to lay eggs.

An Atlantic salmon typically grows about 2.5 feet (75 cm) long.

Birds

Norway has hundreds of species of birds. Some are year-round residents while many others migrate to Africa during the winter. With the cold temperatures and short periods of daylight, the winter months see the fewest birds. Some species, such as

Male king eider ducks are easy to identify by their uniquely colored heads.

eiders and grebes, spend the winter along the coast. At the end of the cold season, many birds—from smaller types such as plovers and starlings to larger birds such as buzzards and hawks—begin returning to Norway. Many congregate along the coastal areas first, while more inland species come a short time later.

Once the temperatures rise and spring is in full bloom, birds come by the thousands to nest and breed. Some birds, like puffins and gannets, nest in cliffsides, while many other birds head for the trees or nest in burrows. In summer, parents tend to hatchlings until they are ready to fly on their own. By September and early October, many birds take flight toward the south once again, often traveling in enormous flocks that all but darken the sky. By the end of November, just about all migrating species are gone until the following year.

National Bird

The white-throated dipper is Norway's national bird. This small, round, brown, gray, and white bird needs fast-running fresh water to feed. The dipper wades and dives into the water, snatching up shrimp, fish, worms, beetles, and other food.

One of the most impressive Norwegian species is the osprey. It is strikingly handsome, usually with a light-colored chest and head in stark contrast to dark wings. Its diet consists almost entirely of fish. The osprey is a good hunter because of

An osprey snatches a fish from the water.

Cloudberries are shaped like raspberries but taste more like apples. In Norway, they're often eaten with cream and sugar as a dessert.

its incredibly sharp eyesight—it can spot a fish just under the water's surface from 100 feet (30 m) above the water. It will then dive down and hover just above its prey for a moment before snatching it.

Plant Life

About a quarter of Norway's land area is forested. Norwegian forests are dominated by cone-bearing trees like spruce and pine, but they also include deciduous trees—those that lose their leaves in the winter—such as ash, birch, and alder. In lower-elevation areas where the climate is milder, particularly

in the southern half of the country, deciduous forests are more common. In these regions there are many birch, ash, oak, holly, elm, and maple trees. On some parts of the coast warmed by the Gulf Stream, palm trees manage to survive.

Berry-producing plants are found throughout the country. Among the most common are blueberries, cloudberries, and lingonberries.

Large areas of tundra are in the north, where temperatures reach the lowest in the country. Tundras are regions where few trees grow because the temperatures are cold and the growing season is short. Instead of trees, Norway's tundra is covered by low-growing shrubs, grasses, and other small plants. Some of these plants produce flowers for a brief period, creating a colorful patchwork on the ground amid the rocky landscape.

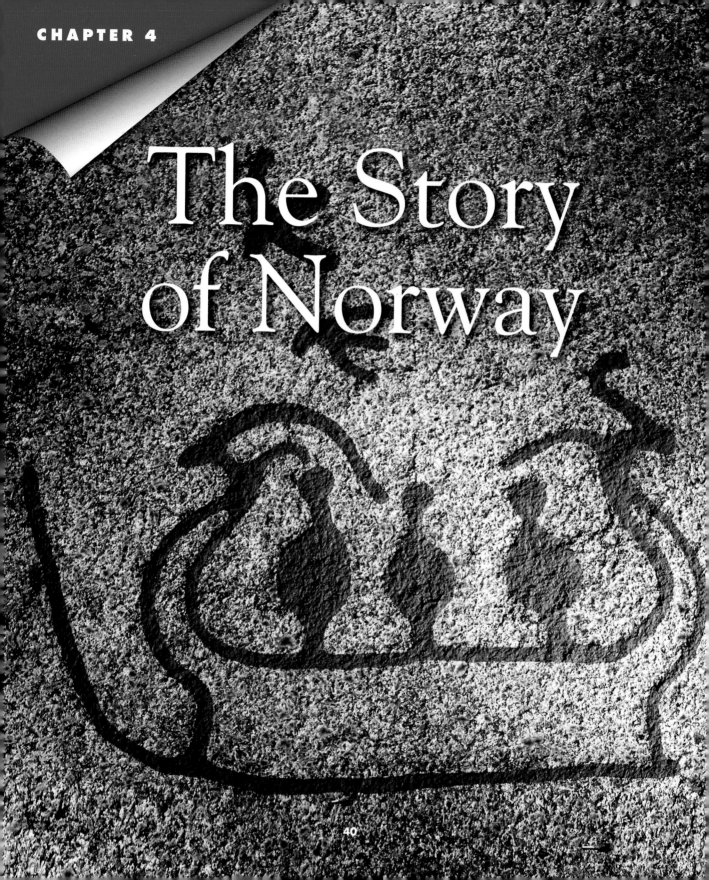

CHAPTER 4

The Story of Norway

PEOPLE FIRST ARRIVED IN WHAT IS NOW NORWAY sometime about 10,000 BCE, after the glaciers from the last ice age retreated, exposing the land. These early settlers came from the south and were drawn by the good hunting and fishing. Coastal areas were preferred for their warmth, but as the glaciers continued to retreat and forests grew in their place, settlers moved farther inland.

By 7500 BCE, people had moved into forested regions well away from the ocean. They were hunter-gatherers, fashioning tools and weapons from wood, stone, and bone. They made tools such as spears and arrows. Some of these early Scandinavian people domesticated dogs. By 3000 BCE, they were making pottery.

Opposite: **Early Scandinavian people sometimes painted images on rocks. This depiction of a hunter in a boat is from at least 2,500 years ago.**

Pottery made by the Corded Ware people. The Corded Ware culture stretched across much of northern and eastern Europe and into Asia.

Changing Culture

A group known as the Corded Ware culture arrived sometime around 2500 BCE. By this time, these people had already settled in many other parts of Europe. They brought an early Indo-European language from which, at least in part, many modern languages evolved, including early Norwegian dialects. The Corded Ware people used wagons and other wheeled vehicles, and there is evidence that they raised animals not only for their meat but also for their milk, fur, hides, and bones. The Corded Ware people may have also introduced the battle-ax, a weapon with one or two curving blades on a long pole. Battle-axes were also likely used for everyday chores such as splitting wood and cutting meat.

In the centuries that followed, people in Scandinavia made further progress in areas such as farming, construction, and toolmaking. Although many of the earliest settlers in the region were nomadic, more and more people built permanent homes and claimed land for farming. Family members built homes near each other. Communities arose with vaguely organized governments. The most successful farmers were looked upon as societal leaders. And as early Norwegians' good fortune increased, so did their interest in other lands.

Viking boats were powered by both sails and oars.

The Vikings

Starting in the late 700s CE, Norwegians began to venture outside their native region in an effort to expand their land

Vikings head ashore in preparation for battle.

holdings. These seafarers became known as the Vikings. They were skilled boatbuilders and sailors, and used longships to explore, trade, and raid. Longships were ideal for long voyages because they were durable. Most were made from oak, one of the hardiest woods available, while the sails were made from wool fabrics. In the winter, Vikings often turned their boats upside down and used them as shelters.

The Vikings were excellent navigators. Braving potentially rough waters, they found their way to distant lands. In some cases, they made settlements and formed colonies.

For example, in the mid-800s, they reached Iceland, a region that was unclaimed and suitable for colonization. In about 980, a young man named Erik the Red left Iceland and explored west, encountering a large island. He returned to Iceland, calling the land to the west Greenland in the hope of persuading people to start a settlement there. In fact, Greenland was much icier and less inviting than Iceland. Other Norse Vikings journeyed to parts of what are now Scotland, England, and Ireland. Some even sailed to northeastern Canada, becoming the first Europeans to set foot in the Americas, hundreds of years before Italian explorer Christopher Columbus crossed the Atlantic Ocean.

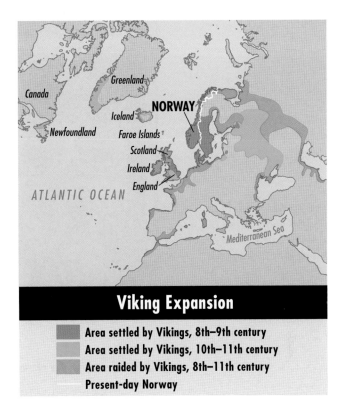

Viking Expansion

- Area settled by Vikings, 8th–9th century
- Area settled by Vikings, 10th–11th century
- Area raided by Vikings, 8th–11th century
- Present-day Norway

The Truth About Vikings

Vikings were typically well-armed and trained in combat. As a result, there is a popular idea today that Vikings were brutal and violent people who raided weaker societies. While there is evidence of Vikings overwhelming towns and villages and making off with treasure, food, and other goods, it is also true that they traded, negotiated, and started settlements.

The Roman Catholic Church named Olaf II a saint shortly after his death. Throughout Norwegian history, he has been considered an important figure of national pride.

Christianity Arrives

The Vikings did not worship a single god. Instead, their religious beliefs included many gods, ranging from spirits living within objects to beings that helped with farming. Over time, however, Christianity was introduced into Norway and replaced the Vikings' pagan religion.

Christianity began spreading in Scandinavia in the 700s but did not have much success in Norway until the 900s. A key figure in the Christianization of Norway was Olaf II Haraldsson, who ruled from 1015 to 1030. He encouraged the spread of Christianity through his kingdom, often by force, and enacted a religious code. By the time Olaf died in 1030, Christianity had become fully rooted in Norwegian culture, with the echoes of paganism fading fast.

Rise and Fall

As Christianity spread, Viking culture declined. By 1100, it was all but gone. During the following 250 years, Norway enjoyed relative peace and prosperity.

But Norway's growth was interrupted by the deadly bubonic plague. The Black Death, as it is called, struck Norway in 1349 and within a few years had killed two-thirds of the population. So many people died that the rulers and government had trouble functioning. The country was devastated.

The Black Death devastated Europe and the Middle East, killing perhaps seventy-five million people in four years.

Akershus Fortress

One of Norway's most celebrated historic landmarks is Akershus Fortress. Built in the late thirteenth century, it served as a stronghold to protect the city of Oslo. It was attacked by Swedish forces in the fourteenth and fifteenth centuries, but was never conquered. In fact, it was never once overrun in its eight-hundred-year existence (although it was surrendered to the Germans along with the rest of the city in 1940 during World War II). Akershus Fortress also served as a prison for much of its existence. Although it is still a military facility today, it is primarily used for official dinners and celebrations.

The Kalmar Union

Norway was closely tied to the neighboring Scandinavian countries of Sweden and Denmark. Following the Black Death, Norway was weak and impoverished, its small popu-

Margaret I of Denmark was the most powerful ruler in Scandinavia for more than thirty years.

lation scattered across the land. As a result, alliances with neighboring countries became even more important. In 1387, Queen Margaret I of Denmark began her reign. She worked to unite the Scandinavian countries, and in 1397, her heir, Erik VII, became king of Denmark, Norway, and Sweden. This was known as the Kalmar Union.

Problems with the alliance began quickly. Norway was weaker than the other countries, and many government appointments went to Danes. The policies put in place tended to benefit Denmark more than Norway. Nevertheless, the Kalmar Union remained intact until 1523, when Sweden broke away. Denmark and Norway, however, remained united.

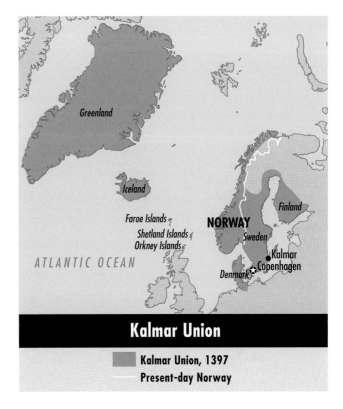

Kalmar Union

Kalmar Union, 1397
Present-day Norway

Growth and Change

In the eighteenth century, Norway enjoyed a period of growth and prosperity as a result of greater international trade and the emergence of new markets. Norway's lumber industry had been important since the 1600s and it continued to expand. Silver and copper mining were also increasing. Yet despite some advances in Norway, political, economic, and intellectual power remained centered in Denmark.

Europe was embroiled in conflict in the early 1800s. Napoleon Bonaparte led the French Empire and its allies in battle against England and its allies. Although Denmark-Norway tried to stay neutral, it was drawn into the Napoleonic Wars on the side of France in 1807. The wars left Norway in economic dismay. Sensing Norway's weakness, Sweden, an ally of England, invaded in 1808, but the Norwegians managed to hold their ground. Nevertheless, Sweden and its allies defeated Napoleon in 1813. In the resulting fallout, Norway was essentially handed to Sweden as a war prize.

Norwegians on a ship leaving for the United States say good-bye to their friends and family on the dock in Oslo.

In the aftermath of the war, Norway's economic recovery was slow. But by the mid-1800s it was enjoying another growth period, with the textile industry on the rise. Mills producing yarns and cloth sprung up around the southern part of the country. Roads and railroads were built. Along with the rise of the nation's industry came an expansion of merchant shipping. These ships carried goods and people around the world. They opened new markets where products could be sold.

The nineteenth century also saw large numbers of Norwegians leaving home, looking for a better life elsewhere. When crops failed, people went hungry, or laborers' jobs were replaced by machines, many Norwegians headed west to the United States and Canada. In the United States, Wisconsin and Minnesota attracted the most Norwegian settlers. They wrote enthusiastic letters to their friends and family back home. These letters encouraged others to follow, so for some time there was a steady flow of Norwegian immigrants into

Norwegians Around the World

Norwegians have migrated to many parts of the world in addition to North America. In the 1600s and 1700s, as many as eighty thousand Norwegians emigrated to the Netherlands and Denmark, mostly for jobs on merchant ships. Trade was robust at this time, and Norwegians found many more opportunities working on ships than working on the land back home.

In Russia, a small settlement of Norwegians was established in the Kola Peninsula starting in 1860. For the next few decades, this group enjoyed relative prosperity and steady contact with their homeland. Troubles for them began in the early twentieth century, however, starting with the Russian Revolution of 1917. During World War II, most of the Norwegians on the Kola Peninsula died of starvation.

Other Norwegian colonies around the world, while relatively small, have fared better. There are Norwegian communities in Australia, South Africa, and Brazil.

the American Midwest and Canada. Between 1840 and 1914, about 750,000 people left Norway, at a time when the country's population was between 1.5 and 2.5 million. Today, about five million Americans and half a million Canadians have some Norwegian ancestry.

Workers' Rights

As industry and trade increased, the middle class grew. Along with their new economic and social standing, many people wanted more representation in public affairs. Those in the

Rows of workers toil at a cigar factory in the late nineteenth century.

ruling class were hesitant to surrender much of their long-held power and influence, and tensions grew. There were attempts made to establish a political party representing the working class toward the end of the 1850s, but they were not successful. Undaunted, workers persisted until, at last, a two-party system was established in 1884, with the Liberal Party representing laborers and the Conservative Party representing the rulers.

In spite of their increased power through political representation, many Norwegian laborers found themselves subjected to highly exploitative and dangerous working conditions at the dawn of the twentieth century. Textile factories, for example, had little in the way of fire protection. Workers were exposed to harmful chemicals. Twelve-hour workdays during the week were common in some places, along with work on Saturday and even Sunday. Pay was low compared to the profits being made by the factory owners.

From workers' growing dissatisfaction came a movement attempting to balance out the inequality between the classes. Laws were enacted creating fairer working conditions and giving working-class people more rights. In 1898, Norway granted all men the right to vote.

Independence and War

By the end of the nineteenth century, Norway had become strong enough both politically and economically to seek independence. In 1905, the Norwegian parliament passed a resolution to formally end Norway's union with Sweden,

To the Pole!

One of the boldest explorers in Norway's history was Roald Amundsen. He was among the first people to visit the continent of Antarctica, and the very first to reach the South Pole. After setting up camp in Antarctica in early 1911, he made preparations, depositing supplies of food along the route, and then waited for ideal conditions for the journey. He and four other men finally made their approach to the South Pole in October 1911. As luck would have it, the weather turned bad soon after they set out, but Amundsen chose not to turn back. He nearly died when a snow bridge collapsed beneath him. In mid-November, the team came to the Transantarctic Mountains, which took nearly two weeks to pass because there was not a clear route across them. They also had to deal with diminishing food supplies, continuing weather difficulties, and snow that covered deep holes in the ice. Falling in would mean almost certain death. But Amundsen and his team pressed on, and on December 14, they became the first people to reach the South Pole. Amundsen erected a Norwegian flag to mark the achievement.

establishing itself as a fully independent nation. Norway then entered another period of rapid industrial growth.

World War I began in Europe in 1914, with Great Britain, France, and Russia leading a group of nations known as the Allies against the Central powers, led by Germany and Austria-Hungary. Although Norway declared itself neutral, it was greatly affected by the war. Norway had one of the largest merchant marine fleets in the world, and the British took over a number of their ships. Many of Norway's ships were then sunk by German submarines. In addition, Norway could no longer trade with Germany, harming its economy further.

When World War II broke out in 1939, Norway again declared itself neutral. But Germany, under the rule of Adolf Hitler and the Nazi Party, quickly gained control of much

of Europe. German forces invaded Norway in April 1940 and took over Oslo and other important cities. The government and the royal family fled to England. Although some Norwegians supported Germany, many others fought the Nazi occupation. They took part in strikes and destroyed German industrial plants in Norway. In addition, the one thousand ships in Norway's merchant fleet were administered out of London, England. Norway's oil tankers, in particular, were vital to the effort to win the war. When Germany was finally defeated in 1945, Norway was once again free.

Nazi troops parade through Oslo in 1940. Hundreds of thousands of German soldiers were stationed in Norway during the occupation to prevent an invasion by Allied forces.

After the War

After the war, Norway's economy grew, with agriculture and industry expanding. By the mid-1960s, new schools, roads, and bridges were being built, progressive government programs were taking root, and industrial markets were booming.

As the twentieth century progressed, the government would come to play a significant role in many major industries, sometimes taking control of them entirely. It also put into place a progressive tax system, taxing the wealthy at a higher rate than people who had less money. With this money, the government could pay for generous social programs, providing health care, education, old-age pensions, and much more to the people of Norway.

An old woman sits with her cat in a barn. In Norway, the average life expectancy is eighty-two years.

The Modern Era

The modern era of Norway's history began in the 1960s, when an American company discovered oil under the ocean floor off the Norwegian coast. An oil industry under Norway's control quickly rose up, which brought large amounts of money into the country. The economy grew, more and more people found jobs, and the standard of living rose.

Norway's growing economy drew more and more immigrants to the country. Some came from Europe. Others came from more distant countries such as Pakistan and Somalia. Today, immigrants and children of immigrants make up 16 percent of the population of Norway.

In recent decades, Norway has experienced economic downturns and cultural changes. But through it all, the oil industry has remained strong. As the twenty-first century progresses, Norway continues to have one of the lowest unemployment rates and strongest economies in Europe.

Terror and Tragedy

In 2011, Norway suffered twin terrorist attacks by a right-wing extremist named Anders Behring Breivik. On the same day, he methodically shot people at a Labor Party youth movement summer camp, killing sixty-nine, and exploded a bomb in Oslo, killing eight. The attacks injured more than three hundred other people. Breivik's actions were the deadliest event in Norway since World War II.

CHAPTER 5

The World of Politics

NORWAY'S GOVERNMENT STRUCTURE IS SIMILAR IN many ways to that of the United States. There are, for example, three branches of government—the executive, the legislative, and the judicial. Norway's leaders act under the authority outlined in their constitution. It was adopted in 1814 and has been revised many times since then. The public chooses most political leaders through free elections. There are several political parties in the Norwegian system, each with its own platform and point of view.

There are also significant differences between the Norwegian and American political systems. For example, in the United States, the head of the executive branch of

Opposite: **A large stone lion sits in front of the building where the Norwegian legislature meets.**

The Flag

Norway's flag consists of a red field with two blue bars, one horizontal and one vertical, creating a cross. Both blue bars are outlined in white. The cross sits off-center, which is known as a Scandinavian cross. Both Denmark and Sweden also use Scandinavian crosses in their flag designs. The design was created by Fredrik Meltzer, a member of Norway's parliament, in 1821 and adopted in May of that year. He chose the colors because they are the colors of the French flag and have come to symbolize liberty.

government—the president—has a great amount of political power and influence. He or she can issue executive orders,

Harald V has been the king of Norway since 1991.

reject bills that have been passed by Congress, and set military strategy. The head of Norway's executive branch—the king—is a largely ceremonial position, with little actual authority.

The Executive Branch

Norway's executive branch is headed by the king. The king of Norway holds some political power, but in order to exercise it he must rely on the Council of State, a group of advisers led by the prime minister, the head of the government. The other members of the council are chosen by the prime minister and are almost always high-ranking government officials.

Also in the executive branch is a group of ministries. These include the Ministries of Defense, Education, Energy, Transportation, and Climate and Environment.

King Harald V

Norway's current monarch is King Harald V, who has held this position since the death of his father, King Olav V, in 1991. Harald was born in Skaugum in 1937 and was forced to flee Norway with his mother and siblings in 1940 when the Nazis invaded during World War II.

In 1968, Harald married Sonja Haraldsen. She is an ordinary Norwegian citizen, rather than a noble, and at the time this was controversial in Norway. They have two children, Märtha and Haakon.

Today, Harald hosts weekly meetings with both the Council of State and the prime minister. He also travels abroad extensively to represent the country.

National Anthem

Norway does not have an official national anthem, but "Ja, Vi Elsker Dette Landet" ("Yes, We Love This Country") is typically used at ceremonies. The lyrics are by Bjornstjerne Bjornson, and the music is by Rikard Nordraak. It was first performed in 1864.

Norwegian lyrics

Ja, vi elsker dette landet,
som det stiger frem,
furet, vaerbitt over vannet,
med de tusen hjem—
elsker, elsker det og tenker
pa var far og mor
og den saganatt som senker
drommer pa var jord.
Og den saganatt som senker,
drommer pa var jord.

Norske mann i hus og hytte,
takk din store Gud!
Landet ville han beskytte,
skjont det morkt sa ut.
Alt, hva fedrene har kjempet,
modrene har grett,
har den Herre stille lempet,
sa vi vant var rett.

Ja, vi elsker dette landet,
som det stiger frem,
furet, vaerbitt over vannet,
med de tusen hjem.
Og som fedres kamp har hevet
det av nod til seir,
ogsa vi, nar det blir krevet,
for dets fred slar leir.

English translation

Yes, we love this country
as it rises forth,
rugged, weathered, above the water,
with the thousands of homes,
love, love it and think
of our father and mother
and the saga-night that lays
dreams upon our earth.
And the saga-night that lays
dreams upon our earth.

Norwegian man in house and cabin,
thank your great God!
The country he wanted to protect,
although things looked dark.
All the fights fathers have fought,
and the mothers have wept,
the Lord has quietly moved
so we won our rights.

Yes, we love this country
as it rises forth,
rugged, weathered, above the sea,
with those thousand homes.
And as the fathers' struggle has raised
it from need to victory,
even we, when it is demanded,
for its peace will encamp (for defense).

The Legislative Branch

Norway's parliament, or lawmaking body, is known as the Storting. Unlike the U.S. Congress, it is a unicameral body, which means it has just one chamber. It has 169 members, who serve four-year terms.

Elections in Norway are very different from those in the United States. Norway is divided into nineteen counties. The ballots indicate the parties with a list of names next to each. These are the candidates from that party, in order of the party's preference. People vote by selecting the party rather than individuals. If a party wins a quarter of the votes

The Norwegian legislature is called the Storting, which means the "great council."

A Norwegian Takes the Lead

During her long career, Norwegian doctor and politician Gro Harlem Brundtland has been a leader at home and around the world. In 1981, Brundtland, a member of the Labor Party, became Norway's first female prime minister. At the time, Norway's economy was struggling, and she served only a few months. She again became prime minister in 1986, and served in that job for most of the following decade.

Brundtland has also had an important career internationally. In 1983, she became the chair of the United Nations World Commission on Environment and Development, which became known as the Brundtland Commission. This commission introduced the concept of "sustainable development," the idea of economic growth and development that protects the natural world. In 1998, Brundtland served as the head of the World Health Organization, battling diseases such as AIDS around the globe. More recently, she has worked on how to respond to the problem of climate change.

in one county, it will be allotted a quarter of that county's seats in Parliament. These seats are filled by the list of names that appeared on the ballot. One hundred fifty members of Parliament are chosen based upon the party chosen at the county level. Another nineteen are based on the votes of the country at large.

In Norway, many different parties vie for power. In 2016, for example, eight different parties held seats in the Storting. Because there are so many parties, no single party usually holds a majority of seats in Parliament. As a result, more than

There is no dominant political party in Norway. Instead, the nation has about eight leading parties, known as parliamentary parties because they get enough votes to win seats in Parliament, and another dozen non-parliamentary parties that do not enjoy as much power.

The most powerful parties are the Labor Party and the Conservative Party. The Labor Party is a more liberal, social democratic party that argues that the government is for the benefit of everyone and should create a fairer, more egalitarian society. The Conservative Party argues for lower taxes and less government involvement in the economy, while also being socially liberal. Together, these two parties usually control more than half the seats in Parliament.

Most of the non-parliamentary groups have little chance of becoming influential. Examples include the Coastal Party, which represents more conservative rural interests, and the Sami People's Party, which works to further the interests of the Sami minority group.

one party must come together in a coalition to choose a prime minister and form a government. In 2013, Conservative Party leader Erna Solberg became prime minister, leading a coalition made up of the Conservative Party, the Progress Party, the Liberal Party, and the Christian People's Party.

The Judicial Branch

The highest court in Norway is called the Supreme Court. A chief justice leads the court, which also includes nineteen other justices. The Supreme Court reviews decisions made in lower courts. Decisions made in the Supreme Court are final. The Supreme Court handles both civil and criminal cases, and it can also rule on whether actions or laws violate the constitution. The number of Supreme Court justices that hear a case varies. Many cases are heard by five justices. If a case could affect existing law, it might be heard by eleven justices. A few cases involve all twenty justices. People appointed to the Supreme Court serve until age seventy.

Norway's National Government

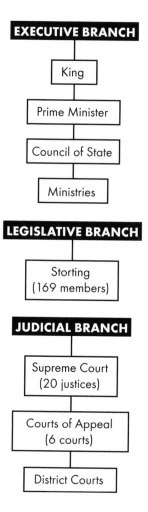

EXECUTIVE BRANCH

King

Prime Minister

Council of State

Ministries

LEGISLATIVE BRANCH

Storting
(169 members)

JUDICIAL BRANCH

Supreme Court
(20 justices)

Courts of Appeal
(6 courts)

District Courts

Below the Supreme Court in Norway are six courts of appeal spread around the country. They review cases tried in district courts, where cases are first heard. Typically in Norway, judges rather than juries determine the outcome of trials.

A Look at the Capital

Norway's capital city is Oslo, which lies along the southern coast. It was likely founded sometime around the year 1000 CE and became the capital in 1299. About fifty years later, however, three-quarters of the city's population was wiped out by the Black Death. Gradually, the city recovered.

Norway's first college was founded in Oslo in 1813, and throughout the nineteenth and twentieth centuries the city became a cultural center as many theaters and museums were founded. Today, it is home to the National Theatre; the National Museum of Art, Architecture, and Design; the Historical Museum; the Viking Ship Museum; and the Norwegian Folk Museum. Oslo is also home to many parks, galleries, lively shopping districts, and excellent restaurants.

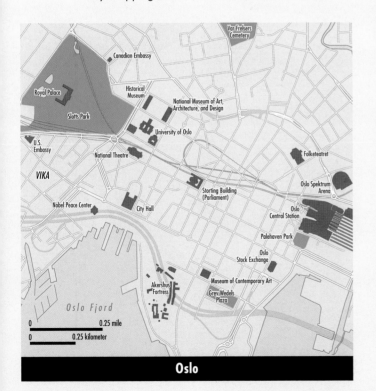

Oslo

Oslo is a center of banking, industry, and trade in Norway. In 2016, it had a population of 660,987, with the urban area having a population of about 1.2 million. Around a quarter of the people in Oslo are immigrants. They come from nearby countries such as Sweden and more distant countries such as Poland, Pakistan, and Somalia. Many other people living in the capital city have moved there from other parts of the country. Oslo is one of the most expensive cities in the world to live in, but it also offers one of the highest standards of living.

CHAPTER 6

Wealth from Oil

NORWAY IS ONE OF THE MOST PROSPEROUS nations, with a high average standard of living. This is largely a result of the discovery of major oil reserves in Norwegian territory under the North Sea in the 1960s. Because Norway has a small population, it has been able to use its wealth from oil to provide excellent benefits and services to its people.

Opposite: **An oil platform rises above the North Sea.**

Oil and Natural Gas

The first significant Norwegian oil reserve was discovered in August 1969 off the country's southwestern coast. This reserve, eventually named the Ekofisk field, was tapped in an arrangement with the American company Phillips Petroleum. Since then, numerous other reserves have been discovered in Norwegian waters, as well as large amounts of natural gas.

By 2014, Norway was producing about 1.9 million barrels of oil a day. This made it the largest oil producer of any European

Norway and the European Union

Norway is one of the few countries in Europe that has not joined the European Union (EU). The EU is a political and economic union that included twenty-eight nations in 2016. The purpose of the union was to allow goods and people to move freely from one country to another, making Europe a single market. In addition, many EU countries also use a common currency, the euro.

Although Norway chose not to join the union, it has a good relationship with the EU. It is a member of the European Free Trade Association and the European Economic Area, which means that goods and services can move between Norway and the EU nations without being taxed. Norway does not adopt all EU laws, especially those concerning agriculture and fishing, yet it does contribute to the EU budget.

nation. Many people believe that oil production in the North Sea has peaked and will decline in the future. Many also believe, however, that the Barents Sea to the north of Norway may hold one of the largest remaining untapped petroleum and natural gas reserves in the world. Many companies are actively searching for oil there now.

The Norwegian government controls the oil industry. It owns a large part of the Norwegian oil company Statoil and gives contracts to other oil companies to explore for oil in Norwegian territory.

Norway is also a major producer of natural gas. By 2013, it was the third-largest producer of natural gas in the world. Much of this gas comes from the vast Troll field west of Bergen.

What Norway Grows, Makes, and Mines

Sheep block a road in southern Norway.

AGRICULTURE (2012)

Sheep	2,223,600 animals
Cattle	861,924 animals
Barley	573,200 metric tons

MANUFACTURING (VALUE OF SALES, 2015)

Machinery and equipment	$19,400,000,000
Food products	$8,400,000
Ships and oil platforms	$7,800,000,000

MINING

Oil (2014)	1,904,000 barrels per day
Natural gas (2015)	122,000,000,000 cubic meters
Iron ore (2012)	3,421,000 metric tons

Agriculture

Agriculture plays a small role in the Norwegian economy, employing only about 3 percent of the workers in the country. Many Norwegian farmers raise livestock. Sheep, cattle, and pigs are the most common animals raised. The cold climate and short growing season limit the kinds of foods that can be grown there. Common crops grown in Norway include barley, potatoes, wheat, carrots, turnips, and cabbages. In some areas, fruits such as cherries and apples are also grown.

Leeks are harvested on a farm near Oslo.

Fishing

Fishing is an important industry along the coast. Large ships head out to sea to catch fish such as cod, haddock, and pollack. In recent years, fish farming has grown to become an important part of the economy in coastal regions. At these fish farms, cod, halibut, wolf fish, and other kinds of fish are raised in enclosures. Today, more than a quarter of the fish harvested in Norway comes from fish farms.

A worker feeds salmon at a fish farm in Norway. Salmon make up about 80 percent of all farmed fish in the country.

Manufacturing and Mining

Much of Norway's manufacturing is related to its oil and fishing industries. Norway's booming energy industry has required businesses to construct offshore oil rigs and drilling equipment. The oil is sent to other parts of the world, which encouraged a revival of Norway's shipbuilding industry. Likewise, most of the fish from Norway are processed before they are sold. Some are salted, smoked, or canned. Others are turned into frozen fish fillets. Norway also produces machinery, paper products, and metals.

Some mining also occurs in Norway. Iron ore and ilmenite, the source of titanium, are found in Norway.

Services

Nearly four out of every five workers in Norway are employed in service industries, which include education, health care, banking, tourism, and much more. Trade is a big part of the economy's service sector. Norway exported just over $100 billion worth of goods in 2015. Leading exports include oil, natural gas, food products such as fish, aluminum, machinery, and electronic

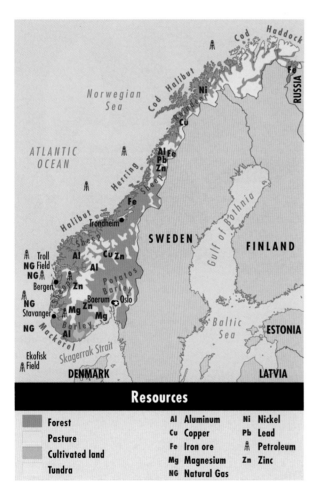

Resources

Forest	Al	Aluminum	Ni	Nickel
Pasture	Cu	Copper	Pb	Lead
Cultivated land	Fe	Iron ore	⚒	Petroleum
Tundra	Mg	Magnesium	Zn	Zinc
	NG	Natural Gas		

equipment. Most of these goods went to the United Kingdom, Germany, Denmark, and the Netherlands.

Major imports include cars, machinery, metals, chemicals, and food products. Norway's major import partners are Sweden, Germany, and China. Many goods also come from the United Kingdom, the United States, and Denmark.

Working Life

Norwegians usually work a forty-hour week, although a shorter workweek has been proposed. Most workers get several weeks of paid vacation time during the year, plus extended leave for special situations such as family births or deaths. Regardless of how much time they have off, Norwegians are highly productive during their work hours.

Money Facts

The basic unit of currency in Norway is the krone. Coins come in values of 1, 5, 10, and 20 kroner. The 1-and 5-kroner coins are notable for having a small hole in the center. Bills have denominations of 50, 100, 200, 500, and 1,000 kroner. Each denomination has a distinct main color. The front depicts a prominent Norwegian and the back shows something associated with that person. The 100-kroner note, for example, is red and features Kirsten Flagstad, one of the greatest opera singers of the twentieth century. The Folketeatret, a concert hall in Oslo, is shown on the back. In 2016, 1 krone equaled 12 U.S. cents, and US$1.00 equaled 8.33 kroner.

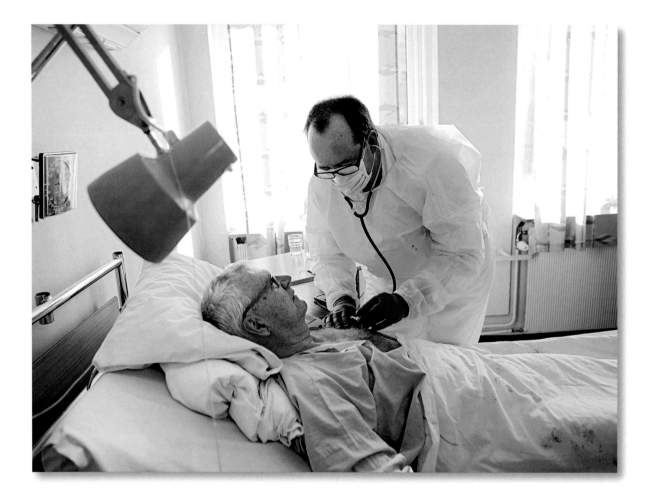

A doctor checks on a patient at a hospital in Oslo. Norway's health care system is considered one of the best in the world.

The average tax rate for most people in Norway is around 40 percent. This tax money pays for the many public services that are provided free of charge to most Norwegians, including those that are extremely expensive in the United States, such as education and health insurance. The working culture in Norway supports family life. Workers are encouraged to spend time with their families rather than devote themselves day and night to their jobs.

As Norway's economy has boomed in recent years, many industries have continued to expand. These include the industries of manufacturing, mining, oil and natural gas, wood and paper products, construction, engineering, health care, communications, and technology. In 2016, the unemployment rate in Norway was less than 5 percent, below that of most other nations.

A technician repairs a computer. Repair work is a service industry.

CHAPTER 7

The People
of Norway

ABOUT 5.2 MILLION PEOPLE MAKE NORWAY THEIR home. Most of them are ethnic Norwegians, people with northern Germanic ancestry.

Four out of every five people in Norway live in an urban area, and the great majority of the population lives in the more developed southern part of the country. Nearly 1 million people live in the Oslo area. But Finnmark, the vast northerly part of the Norwegian mainland, is home to just seventy-five thousand people.

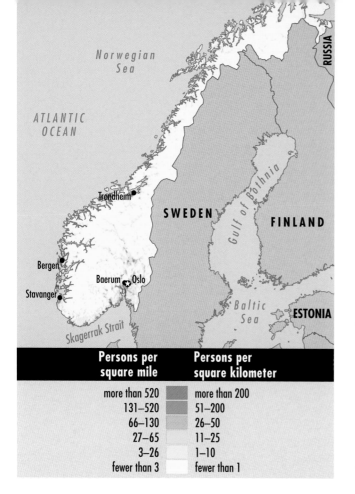

Persons per square mile		Persons per square kilometer
more than 520		more than 200
131–520		51–200
66–130		26–50
27–65		11–25
3–26		1–10
fewer than 3		fewer than 1

Population of Major Cities (2016 est.)	
Oslo	660,987
Bergen	278,120
Trondheim	187,951
Stavanger	132,895
Baerum	122,660

Sami

The native people of northern Norway are called the Sami. The Sami people first arrived in Norway about ten thousand years ago, and as many as sixty thousand live in Norway today. Sami people also live in the Arctic regions of Sweden, Finland, and Russia. Traditionally, the Sami survived by fishing, hunting, and reindeer herding. Although many Sami still live in northern Norway, only a small number of them still herd reindeer today. Others have moved south to Norway's larger urban areas.

There are several different Sami languages, which are related to Finnish. About ten thousand Norwegians speak a Sami language as their first language, and Sami is an official language in several cities in the northern part of the country.

The Sami have suffered discrimination over the years. As Norwegian nationalism rose in the late 1800s, the Sami were pressured to adopt Norwegian culture. By the end of the century, Sami languages were banned in schools and churches. Land in Finnmark, traditional Sami territory that had been used by everyone, was claimed by the government. Sami who wanted to use this land for agriculture had to prove they could speak Norwegian. The government viewed the Sami culture as inferior and had a policy that everyone should adopt Norwegian ways. This policy continued for decades, but by the 1980s, attitudes had changed. In 1989, the Sami Parliament of Norway was created to act on behalf of the Sami people. In 1997, King Harald V apologized to the Sami on behalf of the government.

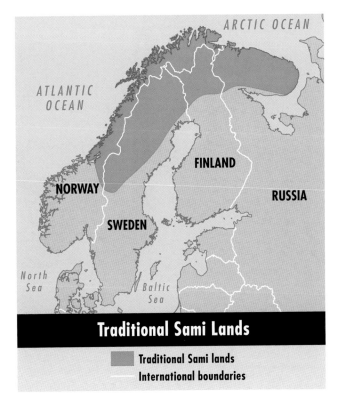

Traditional Sami Lands

■ Traditional Sami lands
— International boundaries

Newcomers

For most of its history, Norway had a fairly homogeneous population, meaning that most people had similar backgrounds. The vast majority of Norwegians were of northern Germanic ancestry. In the twentieth century, more newcomers began arriving, escaping war and violence in their homelands. Jews came from eastern Europe. Later, people arrived from Hungary and Vietnam. More recently, refugees have arrived in Norway from Iraq, Somalia, and Afghanistan. Other immigrants came to Norway for economic reasons. Pakistanis came as part of a guest worker program in the 1970s. In later years, large numbers of Poles and Lithuanians arrived looking for jobs.

In the early 1990s, about 4 percent of Norway's population consisted of immigrants or the children of immigrants. Today,

A Somali refugee walks through the airport in Oslo. More than thirty-five thousand Somalis now live in Norway.

that number has risen to 16 percent. Norway's many large immigrant communities include Poles, Lithuanians, Somalis, Eritreans, Romanians, Turks, Vietnamese, and Iraqis.

Most immigrants to Norway settle in cities. For example, today, about 30 percent of Oslo's population is made up of immigrants and the children of immigrants.

Language

Norwegian is the official language of Norway. It is part of a larger group of Scandinavian languages that also includes Danish, Swedish, Faroese, and Icelandic. Norwegian bears many similarities to Danish and Swedish. They are so closely related that a speaker of one of these languages can often be fully understood by a speaker of another. Modern Faroese and Icelandic, however, are no longer so close and cannot be understood by Norwegian speakers.

In spite of Norway's relatively small population, there are many dialects of Norwegian with varying vocabulary, accents, and grammar, depending largely on the region in which they are spoken. The nation does not have an enforced or even encouraged form of Norwegian, so there is little in the way of uniformity. Nevertheless, most Norwegians have no trouble

Oslo has become a diverse city in recent decades. Many Muslim immigrants live in the neighborhood of Gronland (below).

understanding one another. A person's dialect is an easy way for a Norwegian to identify where a person is from.

Norway has two official written versions of Norwegian—Bokmal and Nynorsk. Bokmal is of Danish origin. Danish was the written language used by Norwegians from the 1500s until the 1800s. During much of this time, Norway was either under the control of Denmark or in union with another neighboring country. By the later 1800s, Norway was experiencing grow-

A road sign in the Svalbard Islands warns drivers of snowmobile traffic.

ing nationalistic pride that resulted in Norwegian independence in 1905. From then on, many Norwegians wanted to forge a more individual national identity. This campaign was reflected in a resistance to the Danish-based Bokmal language and a rise in popularity of Nynorsk, which was considered more purely Norwegian. Today, Bokmal is used by about 85 percent of the population as its primary written form. Most of the rest of the population can write in both Bokmal and Nynorsk. Although more people use Bokmal, Nynorsk has widespread support. Most government employees are required to be fluent in both, and many forms of media are offered to the public in both written forms.

Common Norwegian Words and Phrases

Norwegian	English
Ja	Yes
Nei	No
Vaer sa snill	Please
Takk	Thank you
Vaer sa god	You're welcome
Unnskyld	Excuse me
Beklager	I am sorry
God morgen	Good morning
God kveld	Good evening
God natt	Good night
Hvordan har du det?	How are you?
Det er sa hyggelig a treffe deg.	I am very glad to meet you.
Snakker du engelsk?	Do you speak English?

Education

In Norway, the school year starts in the middle of August and ends in late June. This year is divided into two terms. Students get a long break from mid-December to early January between the two terms.

Children in Norway must attend school starting at age six and going until at least age sixteen. Students first attend primary school, which runs from grades 1 to 7. Primary education

Young people gather around a desk at a school in Norway. For Norwegian teenagers, the school day typically lasts six or seven hours.

includes topics such as math, science, history, geography, and social studies. All Norwegians are required to learn English. Because Norwegians start learning English in grade 1, most have superb English skills by the time they are grown.

Religion is also taught in primary school. Although Christianity is the main focus, in recent years, basic teachings about other religions, including Judaism, Buddhism, and Islam, have been added. Most schools also have classes in subjects such as art, music, and theater. Students do not receive grades during primary school, but their parents get regular reports and are required to review their work. Students who struggle receive extra instruction.

Following primary school comes lower secondary school, which lasts from grades 8 to 10. During lower secondary school, students begin to seriously consider what they'd like to do for a career. They are allowed to take elective classes and should begin making choices based on their interests and future. Their performance at this level also determines whether they qualify for certain types of higher education. Upper secondary school lasts for three years and is comparable to high school in the United States. The grading system in both lower and upper secondary school uses numbers, with a 6 being the best and a 1 being the worst. A 2 is the lowest grade a student can receive and still pass.

Norwegian students are not required to attend upper secondary school, but it is necessary in order for them to pursue many careers. There are two general paths of study in upper secondary school. The first consists of general studies, which can steer a student toward a university-level education upon graduation. The second is more vocational in nature, with two years of in-school training followed by two years of on-the-job training that is like an apprenticeship.

Most universities in Norway are publicly funded and free to students. The nation's oldest and most prestigious university is the University of Oslo, which was established in 1811. It serves about twenty-seven thousand students. For many years, it was the largest institution of higher education in Norway, but the Norwegian University of Science and Technology now holds that title. This university, which has several campuses, serves about thirty-nine thousand students.

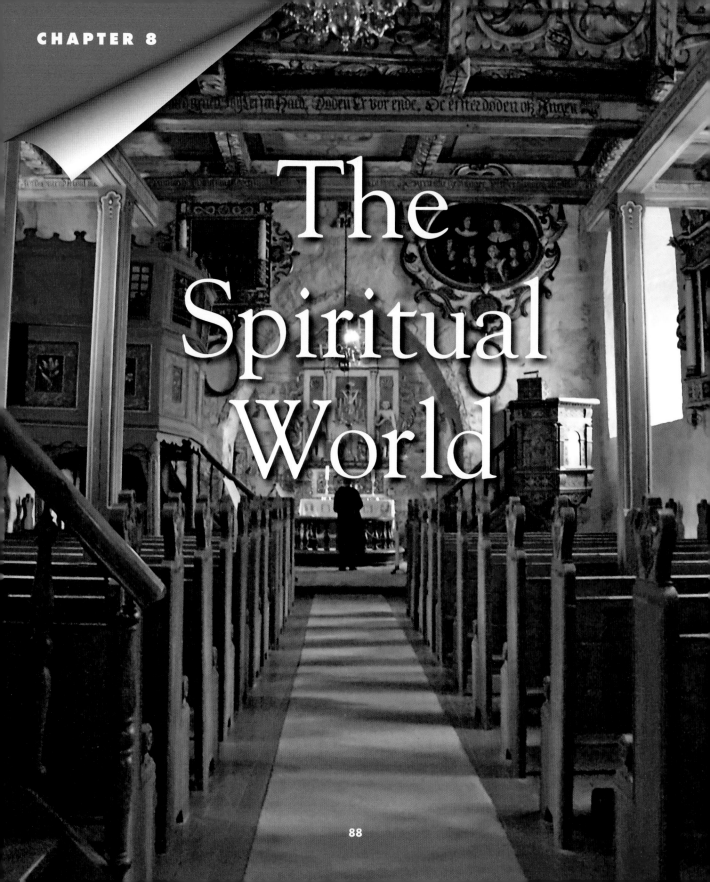

CHAPTER 8

The Spiritual World

THE HISTORY OF RELIGION IN NORWAY CAN BE DIVIDED into three distinct eras—pagan, Catholic, and Protestant. Protestantism is the dominant religion in Norway, and the main Protestant church there is the Evangelical Lutheran Church. Although most Norwegians are officially members of this church, religion plays little or no role in their lives.

Opposite: **The Dale Church in Luster, in central Norway, was built sometime around 1240.**

The Pagan World

Norse paganism began thousands of years ago. What people know of it today is drawn from both archaeological evidence and written accounts that were made many years after the pagan era. In paganism, people worship more than one god. Norse pagans worshipped ancestors who had passed away, minor gods who controlled elements of nature that could help or harm farming, and powerful deities who oversaw life, healing, and death.

A carving depicts a scene from the Norse epic of Siegfried.

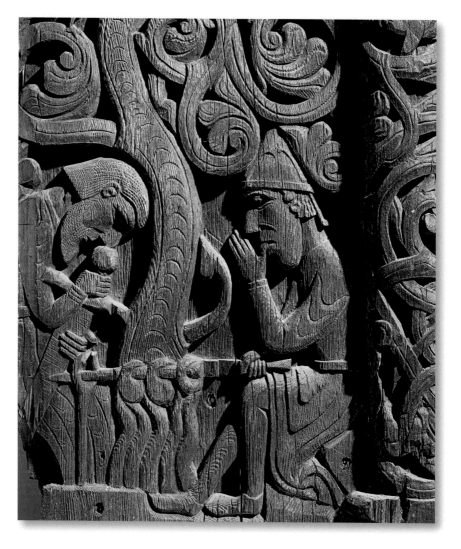

Worship during the pagan era did not typically occur in buildings such as churches. Instead, many rituals were performed outdoors, at sites that were deemed holy and marked off with rocks and tree branches. There were generally no priests or other holy men. Anyone could perform a pagan service, but those people with the greatest authority in each village usually oversaw them. Deities were depicted in various forms, from small items such as jewelry to large statues. The deities included a group called wights. The wights did not have names and were not considered to have the power of the great gods, but still had influence over local peoples. People feared their wrath and practiced ways to either get in their favor or avoid them if they had been angered. Wights were believed to live in natural surroundings such as forests and rivers, and those who feared them would bring offerings so as to assure their kindness.

Norse Mythology

The mythology of Norway began to form prior to the pagan period of Norse history and continued long after the arrival of Christianity. Much of it is Germanic in origin. It is characterized by epic tales of powerful and warring gods as well as stories of heroic human figures.

Norse mythology takes place in what is called the Nine Homeworlds. In these worlds live a variety of figures, including elite gods such as Odin and Thor, elf races such as the Dokkalfar and Ljosalfar, and people who are condemned to suffering after death in a place of darkness and unceasing cold. These nine worlds are said to be interconnected by a tree known as the Yggdrasil. The Yggdrasil is a meeting place for the most powerful of gods and is home to fabled creatures such as dragons. Its roots and branches extend into the heavens as well as into the Well of Mimir. Mimir is a Norse god of wisdom, and his well is filled with knowledge.

Christianity Arrives

Christianity arrived in Scandinavia in the 700s, slowly taking root in Norway until the mid- to late 900s. Conversions to Christianity increased under Olaf Tryggvason, who was crowned King Olaf I in 995. After being wounded in battle, Olaf I became a staunch Christian. He committed himself to establishing Christianity throughout Norway and eliminating paganism. Olaf I sometimes used brutal methods to achieve this, such as burning pagan temples and torturing or killing pagans who would not convert to Christianity. He also used these harsh approaches in lands that Norwegians colonized, such as Iceland and Greenland.

Olaf I died in battle in the year 1000, and in 1015 Olaf II Haraldsson became king. He continued Olaf I's campaign of Christianization. He built churches and integrated Christian beliefs as part of national laws and policies. Like Olaf I, Olaf II used violent means to force people to convert. Olaf II was named a saint after his death and is now considered the patron saint of Norway.

In this scene, Olaf II is shown converting a group of Norwegians to Christianity.

Nidaros Cathedral

Nidaros Cathedral in the city of Trondheim is built over the burial site of Saint Olaf, the patron saint of Norway. Work on the building began in 1070, and it has been damaged and restored many times since then. At the time it was constructed, Nidaros Cathedral was a Roman Catholic church. But when Norway became Protestant in the 1500s, so did the cathedral. The church is renowned for its beauty and abundant sculptures of saints and other religious figures. It is the northernmost medieval cathedral in the world.

The Rise of Protestantism

Roman Catholicism was the dominant religion in western Europe in the early 1500s. The church was wealthy and politically powerful. Some people believed many church officials were greedy and corrupt. They wanted to reform the church, so this movement became known as the Reformation. One of the leaders of the Reformation was a German priest named Martin Luther. In 1517, Luther wrote a tract known as the Ninety-five Theses, which outlined his complaints against the Catholic Church. This helped spark the Reformation, which was the beginning of a major branch of Christianity called Protestantism. In time, Protestantism would develop several different denominations, including Lutheranism, Anglicanism, Calvinism, Methodism, and Pentecostalism.

In 1536, while Norway was under the rule of Denmark, Danish king Christian III converted his kingdom from Catholicism to Lutheranism. The changes that followed were rapid and forceful. Lutheran authorities seized Catholic

property, outlawed Catholic practices, and banished Catholic leaders. The government helped fund the construction of new Lutheran churches and the spread of Lutheran teachings. Danish versions of the Bible were distributed, and Lutheran ideas were taught in schools.

In time, other forms of worship were outlawed, making evangelical Lutheranism the official religion of the country. By the mid-1800s, these laws were relaxed, but the right to religious freedom was not added to the constitution until 1964. In 2012, Norway changed its constitution again, ending the Evangelical Lutheran Church's status as the official state church.

Norwegian Lutherans attend a funeral in the 1800s.

Worshippers fill a church on a Sunday morning in Oslo.

Religion Today

Evangelical Lutheranism remains the leading religion in Norway. About three out of every four Norwegians belong to the Evangelical Lutheran Church, which is also known as the Church of Norway. The official statistics, however, are artificially high because any child born in Norway who has one parent who is a member of the Evangelical Lutheran Church is automatically considered a member.

Roman Catholics make up about 2 percent of the Norwegian population. A large percentage of them are immigrants. People who have moved from Poland make up the largest group of Catholics in Norway. There are also large numbers of Catholics of Lithuanian and Vietnamese backgrounds.

Religion in Norway (2013)	
Church of Norway	82%
Other Protestant	4%
Muslim	2%
Roman Catholic	2%
Other	10%

Norway is also home to small numbers of Christians who belong to other denominations. Among the largest of these other groups are Pentecostals, Orthodox, Jehovah's Witnesses, Methodists, and Baptists.

Muslims account for about 2 percent of Norway's population. Most Muslims in Norway are immigrants, with many coming form Pakistan, Somalia, Iraq, Afghanistan, and Bosnia. Most live in Oslo and nearby areas, but Muslims live throughout the country. Tromso, in northern Norway, is home to the world's northernmost mosque, or Muslim house of worship.

Norwegian Muslims praying in Oslo. In the Muslim tradition, people pray five times a day, always facing in the direction of Mecca, Saudi Arabia, the holiest city in Islam.

A small number of people of other faiths, such as Buddhism, Hinduism, and Judaism, also live in Norway.

A large number of Norwegians are atheists, meaning they do not believe in God. Even among those who declare themselves part of the Lutheran Church of Norway, most are not active in the church and many are not religious at all. Norway is, in fact, one of the least religious nations in Europe.

A rabbi takes part in a service at a synagogue in Oslo. The capital city has the largest Jewish population in Norway.

Sami Religion

Traditional Sami religion focused on nature. The Sami believed that different spirits ruled different parts of the natural word, such as the sun or thunder, and that everything had a soul, including animals, plants, and objects. In the traditional Sami world, shamans were believed to be able to communicate with the spirits. The shamans would use chanting and drumming to go into trances, during which they believed they could enter the spirit world.

After the Evangelical Lutheran Church became the dominant church in Norway, attempts were made to convert the Sami to Christianity. In the 1600s, a church was built in Varanger, in the traditional Sami region of Finnmark. Although the Sami resisted at first, most eventually became Christian. Even today, however, some still follow their traditional religion.

Young Sami men wearing traditional clothing are blessed by a minister.

CHAPTER 9

Arts and Sports

NORWAY'S LITERARY HISTORY STRETCHES BACK AS far as the 800s. In the earliest days, Norse writers used an old form of writing called a runic alphabet. By the eleventh century, however, as Norway had become Christian, the runic alphabet was replaced by the Latin alphabet that was used throughout western Europe and is still used today.

Opposite: **This stone with runic writing and an image of a knight dates back to about 500 CE.**

Literature

Poetry was the first form of literature in Norway. Eyvindr Finnsson, a poet from the 900s, worked in the court of Haakon the Good. Although his work seemed to capture the spirit of

During Viking times, people told heroic tales about their past.

the times, he was often referred to as a *skaldaspillir* (spoiler), which meant that his material drew on existing poetry. He often wrote about celebrated historical events.

By the 1100s, some Norse writers were telling stories in forms other than poetry. Some people wrote narratives about history, which were intended to both educate and entertain. Much of Norse mythology was also written down, in part to counteract efforts by missionaries to replace it with Christian teachings.

From the late fourteenth to the early nineteenth centuries, Norway produced little literature. Celebrated nineteenth-century Norwegian playwright Henrik Ibsen later called this period the "four hundred years of darkness." During this time, Norway was in a union with Denmark, which was the more dominant culture. It all but smothered Norway's literary output with its own. When Norway separated from Denmark in the early 1800s, Norway's literary output grew, along with a new revolutionary spirit and national pride. One of the key figures at this time was poet, playwright, and historian Henrik

Playwright Henrik Ibsen is sometimes called the Father of Realism.

Wergeland, whose works inspired a new generation of young authors. Also emerging during this period was an attempt to forge an individual Norwegian language, Nynorsk, led by linguist Ivar Aasen.

From the twentieth century to today, Norway's literary culture has continued to grow and flourish. In his plays, Henrik Ibsen ignored issues of nationalism and focused instead on realistic drama. In works such as *A Doll's House* and *Hedda*

Ivar Aasen was a self-taught linguist. By studying a variety of Norwegian dialects, he created the written version of Nynorsk, "New Norwegian."

Sigrid Undset is best known for her three-volume novel, *Kristin Lavransdatter*, which was published from 1920 to 1922. The books are renowned for vividly evoking the Middle Ages.

Gabler, he looked deep into the reality of family life, analyzing it with a critical eye. Ibsen is considered one of the world's greatest playwrights.

Poetry also became more modern in the early 1900s. This period saw three Norwegian writers awarded the Nobel Prize in Literature, the world's highest literary honor. Bjornstjerne Bjornson received the award in 1903 for his dynamic poetry. Knut Hamsun won the prize in 1920 for his decades of exploration of the human condition that culminated in the 1917 novel *Growth of the Soil*. And Sigrid Undset was awarded the Nobel Prize in 1928 for a group of three historical novels written from the perspective of a woman living in Scandinavia in the Middle Ages.

This ancient Norwegian horn is made from the horn of a goat. Finger holes have been drilled into it. By covering and uncovering them, a musician can change the sound.

Norwegian literature took a dark turn in the second half of the twentieth century. Jens Bjorneboe, for example, wrote novels that focused on the nature of evil. More recently, Karl Ove Knausgaard has earned great acclaim for his series of six autobiographical novels, called *My Struggle*, which delve into everyday life in minute detail.

Music

Music has been a part of Norway since its very beginning. Early Norse writings mentioned music, and archaeologists have found ancient instruments there. Many were wind instruments made of brass or wood. They were likely used not only to play music but also for war calls and to herd livestock.

Norse folk music arose out of Germanic music. In the past, the folk songs were typically accompanied by traditional dance. One of the most commonly used instruments in Norwegian folk music is the fiddle, or violin. Other stringed instruments such as zithers and dulcimers are also popular, as are flutes and simple horns.

A Norwegian classical music movement began in the 1600s, but did not begin to gain international influence until

A fiddle is a common instrument in traditional Norwegian folk music.

Norwegian soul and jazz singer Miss Tati performs in Bergen. Many different kinds of music are popular in Norway.

the mid-1800s. Composers emphasized Norway's unique national identity as well as an expressive, romantic quality. One of the most important figures during this period was Edvard Grieg, who incorporated elements of Norwegian folk music in his compositions. Many of his pieces are still performed around the world.

The modern musical scene in Norway is similar to that found throughout Europe. Artists specialize in any number of genres, including country, hip-hop, blues, rock, pop, metal, and jazz. Norwegian jazz has grown considerably in recent decades, with innovative musicians forging new sounds by mixing jazz with other forms such as electronica and world music. Oslo is the center of Norway's modern jazz scene.

Film

The Norwegian film industry has existed since the early twentieth century. One of the leading figures in the industry's earliest days was Tancred Ibsen, grandson of the playwright Henrik Ibsen. Tancred Ibsen was in the airline business when he visited the United States in 1923. While in Los Angeles, California, he learned the ways of the filmmaking world. Ibsen returned to Norway and spent the next two decades directing and producing dramas similar to those made in Hollywood. Many of them were enormously popular in his home country.

Tancred Ibsen directed many movies starting in the 1930s. These include *Valfangare* (*Love, Men, and Harpoons*), shown below, from 1939.

Despite Ibsen's output, Norway did not have a large film industry in the 1900s. It wasn't until the 2000s that Norwegian film production began to grow significantly. Major films of recent years include *Max Manus* (2008), about the Norwegian resistance to the Nazi occupation during World War II, and *Headhunters* (2011), a thriller set in the world of big business and modern art.

Norwegian actors dress as German soldiers during the filming of *Max Manus* in Oslo in 2008.

Art

Norwegian art has a long history dating back to Viking times. Vikings were accomplished artisans. Their sculpture, jewelry, and other objects featured intricate carvings. They also carved decorations on everyday items such as boats, axes, stone markers, doors, and helmets. Many of these items have been discovered by archaeologists and retain much of their beauty.

Landscape painting blossomed in the early 1800s in Norway. It featured idyllic scenes of snowy mountains and quaint farm life. Norwegian artists reflected the pride they felt in their home in these paintings, now that they were separated from Denmark and free of Danish rule. The mid-nineteenth

The prows of Viking ships often featured intricately carved figures, such as this snake head.

Into the Depths

Perhaps no Norwegian painter has gained greater fame than Edvard Munch. Born on a farm in December 1863, Munch became interested in art as a young child. He was out of school for long periods because of illness, and he would lie in bed and draw pictures. He studied engineering for a while in his teens, but soon turned to painting full time. Munch experimented with a variety of styles while at the Royal School of Art and Design in what is now Oslo. He continued to experiment while living in Paris, France, and Berlin, Germany, until finally settling on the expressionist approach that would characterize his later work. Munch's most recognized piece is *The Scream*, which portrays a suffering figure with its hands on the sides of its head, set against a vivid backdrop. There are, in fact, four versions of this famed work—a pair of pastels from 1893 and 1895, and a pair of paintings from 1893 and 1910. While most people interpret *The Scream* as a perfect rendering of human anxiety, Munch called it a more general study of the human soul.

century saw the rise of an impressionistic period, with artists painting edgier scenes and urban environments. In the early twentieth century, artists such as Edvard Munch were part of a movement called expressionism, in which artists did not create realistic depictions of a scene but rather painted their emotional responses to it.

Sports

Norwegians love sports, and many make the most of their cold, snowy climate by taking part in the popular activities of ice hockey, snowmobile racing, tobogganing, and skating. Skiing is perhaps the most beloved sport in Norway. Norwegians are proud of their long history of skiing, and they invented the sport of ski jumping. Both of these stories can be explored at the Holmenkollen Ski Museum in Oslo.

Because of the popularity of skiing and other winter sports, Norway has done spectacularly well in the Winter Olympics. Norwegians have won more medals at the Winter Olympics than people from any other nation, taking home 239 medals, 118 of them gold, by 2014. In fact, the three most successful

A Norwegian ski jumper soars through the air. Some of the world's top ski jumpers have flown more than 800 feet (244 m) in a single jump.

Ole Einar Bjoerndalen races across the snow during a biathlon event.

Winter Olympians in history are all Norwegians. Ole Einar Bjoerndalen won thirteen medals in biathlon, a sport that combines shooting and cross-country skiing, between 1998 and 2014. Cross-country skier Bjorn Daehlie took home twelve medals between 1992 and 1998. Marit Bjorgen, also a cross-country skier, has won more medals at the Winter Olympics than any other woman. Her ten medals include six gold.

Norway has twice hosted the Winter Olympics, in 1952 at Oslo and in 1994 at Lillehammer. Norwegians performed particularly well in the 1994 winter games. That year they won twenty-six medals, ten of them gold.

Norway has also made its mark over the years in the Summer Olympics, winning a total of 152 medals by 2016. One of these medalists was Grete Waitz, the first woman to run the marathon, a 26-mile (42 km) road race, in less than two and a half hours. Waitz was one of the most successful marathoners in history. She won the New York City marathon nine times, more than any other runner.

The Youngest Champion

If chess is a sport, then Norway's Magnus Carlsen is the finest athlete on the planet. At present, he is the game's reigning world champion. Born in Tonsberg in 1990, Carlsen showed a natural genius for puzzles as a small child and exhibited tremendous chess skills soon after learning the game. He achieved a grandmaster rating—the highest title in chess—at the age of thirteen. He was the third-youngest person to become a grandmaster.

Carlsen's opponents found his aggressive style of play unpredictable. Soon after reaching grandmaster status, Carlsen defeated former champion Anatoly Karpov and scored a draw against Garry Kasparov, who at the time was the highest-rated player in the world. In 2013, he faced off against Viswanathan Anand for the World Championship, which Anand had held since 2007. Carlsen won the match in ten games and has retained the title ever since. He has also replaced Kasparov as the world's highest-rated player and is considered one of the best players in history.

CHAPTER 10

The Norwegian Way

NORWEGIANS HAVE A REPUTATION FOR TREATING all people equally. They're straightforward, polite, and helpful. To outsiders, they may seem to keep a cool distance from people they don't know. For example, if a visitor asks a Norwegian, "Where is the nearest hotel?" he or she may simply point or give the address and then walk away. Most Norwegians like to get right to the point, without wasting a lot of time, but they eventually drop their guard, becoming warm and friendly.

Opposite: **Grandparents and their grandchildren enjoy a trip on a fjord in the Lofoten Islands.**

Family Life

The family is one of the fundamental building blocks of Norwegian society. It is supported on every front, including by private companies and the government. Thus, a strong family life is greatly encouraged and embraced by most of the people who live in Norway.

A mother pulls her child across the snowy ground in Norway.

The typical family in Norway has changed over the years. When the nation was largely agricultural and most people lived in rural areas, families tended to be large. Extended family members often lived in the same home or very close by. As Norway became more industrialized, many people moved to cities to find work and a better way of life. In the cities, with more expenses and less space, people had fewer children. Today, most families in Norway consist of parents and one or two children. Many Norwegians remain close to their extended families, visiting when they have the chance.

The government supports families at every turn. When a child is born, both mothers and fathers are granted paid leave from their jobs, so they can take care of their child and develop a close and healthy relationship with him or her. Mothers get forty-six weeks of paid leave after the birth of their child—that's nearly eleven months.

In Norwegian families, mothers and fathers share everyday duties. Both men and women routinely cook dinner and wash clothes. There is a strong emphasis on equality between the sexes. Most women who are mothers have careers, and sometimes the mother and father will work alternating schedules so one of them can always be home with their children. If their

A father and his children prepare a meal. Most Norwegians prioritize time with their family over work.

Children play with a parachute at a Norwegian preschool.

schedules overlap, parents have many options for putting their children in day care and after-school care, most of which is paid for by the government.

Children are encouraged from an early age to think for themselves and develop a degree of independence so that they do not rely on their parents forever. Self-sufficiency is seen as a valuable trait, one that encourages children to be confident, obtain early achievement, and have high self-esteem. As a result, many young Norwegians seem more mature than young adults in many other parts of the world.

Norway also has an excellent health care system, which contributes to the long average life of Norwegians. Women in Norway can expect to live to be eighty-four, while men live an average of eighty years.

Birth, Marriage, and Death in Norway

Having a baby is a highly anticipated event in Norway. During the pregnancy, the mother is given a lot of time away from work to concentrate on staying healthy and getting her home ready for the child. Once labor begins, Norwegian health care workers place an emphasis on using natural means to bring the infant into the world. To manage the pain of childbirth, they prefer using techniques such as massage and yoga rather than the drugs that are common in some other nations.

Many Norwegian marriage customs are similar to those in the United States: The bride usually wears a white dress, the groom often wears a tuxedo, and the ceremony is held in either a church or a local government hall. But there are differences between Norwegian and American weddings as well. Traditional Norwegian weddings sometimes feature a procession that is led by one or two fiddle players in colorful clothing. Next in line come the bride and groom, then their parents, bridesmaids and groomsmen, the ring bearer and flower girl, and finally all the other guests. In small towns, this procession may walk from the bride's house all the way to the site of the service. Typically, weddings in Norway are fairly small, with most including only family and a few close friends. Dinner and dancing follow the ceremony.

Funeral customs in Norway are similar to those in the United States. A service is held for friends and family, usually at a local church, and then the deceased is either buried or cremated. Sometimes the ashes are buried a few days later, with only a small, intimate group attending this service. Following a coffin burial, attendees will gather at someone's home, where food and drink will be served.

Food

Much of the Norwegian diet today is based on foods that have formed the staple of meals for centuries. There is a particular emphasis on meats and fish. Standard meats such as beef, chicken, and pork are common, but many dishes also feature duck, rabbit, moose, and reindeer, all animals found in Norway's wilderness. Meats might be roasted or pan-fried. They can be prepared in stews, as sausages and chops, and in pies and cakes. Norwegians enjoy eating many kinds of fish, including cod, herring, salmon, mackerel, brisling, and trout. These can be prepared in a wide variety of ways, including poached, fried, stewed, boiled, broiled, salted, or pickled. Smoking is one of the most popular ways to preserve and present fish in Norway. The fish is salted, cured, and left in a cold smoker until the smoke flavor penetrates deep.

Stews and soups featuring ingredients such as meatballs, mutton, potatoes, and carrots are popular in Norway.

Popular side dishes in Norway feature vegetables such as potatoes, carrots, and onions. Fresh local ingredients are prized.

Bread with cheese is also frequently served. Bread is, in fact, a major part of the average Norwegian diet. Whole wheat and sourdough are common varieties. Open-faced sandwiches with meat and cheese are popular lunches and snacks.

Many delicious desserts are made in Norway. Some are as simple as berries and cream. A popular treat is *krumkake*, which means "bent cake." It is a waffle cookie that is rolled up and

Bread with salmon or meat is a common lunch in Norway.

Krumkaker are made with a krumkake iron that creates a decorative pattern on the waffle cookie.

sometimes filled with whipped cream. *Julekake* is frequently eaten during the Christmas season. It is a bread filled with raisins and other candied fruit, along with spices such as cardamom.

Norway is one of the leading consumers of coffee in the world. Coffee is not simply drunk as a morning pick-me-up to help shake off the previous night's sleep. It is also a staple in social situations.

Kringla

One of the many cookies made at Christmastime in Norway is *kringla*. Have an adult help you make these delicious treats.

Ingredients

3 ½ cups flour

1 tablespoon baking powder

1 teaspoon baking soda

½ cup butter

1 ½ cups sugar

2 cups sour cream

1 teaspoon vanilla

3 egg yolks

Directions

Combine the flour, baking powder, and baking soda in a medium-size bowl. Soften the butter in a microwave oven or in a pot on the stove over low heat. In a second, large bowl, combine the softened butter and the sugar. Mix the sour cream and vanilla in with the butter-sugar mixture. Crack the eggs and separate the egg yolks from the egg whites. Add the yolks to the mixture. Slowly add the dry ingredients to the butter-sugar mixture, combining thoroughly. Then cover the bowl of dough with plastic wrap, put it in the refrigerator, and chill overnight.

The next day, preheat the oven to 400°F. To make the cookies, take a piece of dough and roll it into a long rope shape about 1 foot (30 centimeters) long. Form the rope into a pretzel shape and place it on a cookie sheet. Repeat until all the dough is used. Bake the cookies for 5 minutes. Enjoy!

The Stiff Witch

One of the most delightful games children play in Norway is related to the popular game of tag in the United States. It is called *stiv heks*, or "stiff witch." One person is selected as the witch, and the others try to keep away from that person. If the witch touches another player, that person has to freeze in a standing position with arms out and legs spread apart. The frozen player can only unfreeze if another player crawls between their legs and out the other side before being touched by the witch. If the witch freezes everyone, he or she wins.

Good Times

Like people everywhere, Norwegians like to relax and have fun. Many Norwegian families own second homes, located in the mountains or on the coast along a fjord. Some houses are kept in a family for many generations. They are often simple in design and construction and sometimes have no electricity or running water. But it is the simplicity that draws people to them. It is common for those who own fjord houses to also own a boat and spend time sailing. Fishing is popular, as is gathering crabs and clams. Other people enjoy simply exploring the waters, dropping anchor in order to dive and swim. During the summer, dozens of boats sometimes fill harbors.

Norwegians enjoy dining out, often in large groups of friends or family. A night out might include strolling through the shopping districts or a local park. Many Norwegians like to walk as

Friends relax over coffee at a café in Stavanger.

a way to relax and get exercise, and for recreation they also enjoy watching and playing sports. Norwegians are fond of classic board games such as chess and checkers, and love modern video games as well. They take pleasure in the simple joys of life. For many, there is nothing better than sitting in a café, chatting with friends over a hot cup of coffee.

National Holidays

January 1	New Year's Day
March or April	Maundy Thursday
March or April	Good Friday
March or April	Easter Monday
May 1	Labor Day
May 17	Constitution Day
May or June	Ascension Day
May or June	Whit Monday
December 25	Christmas Day
December 26	Boxing Day

Timeline

NORWEGIAN HISTORY		WORLD HISTORY	
The first people arrive in what is now Norway.	10,000 BCE		
The Corded Ware culture is established in the region.	2500 BCE	ca. 2500 BCE	The Egyptians build the pyramids and the Sphinx in Giza.
		ca. 563 BCE	The Buddha is born in India.
		313 CE	The Roman emperor Constantine legalizes Christianity.
		610	The Prophet Muhammad begins preaching a new religion called Islam.
The Vikings begin exploring beyond Scandinavia.	Late 700s CE		
The Vikings establish a colony on Iceland.	Mid-800s		
Christianity begins to spread in Norway.	900s		
The Vikings reach Newfoundland, in what is now Canada.	ca. 1000	1054	The Eastern (Orthodox) and Western (Roman Catholic) Churches break apart.
		1095	The Crusades begin.
		1215	King John seals the Magna Carta.
		1300s	The Renaissance begins in Italy.
		1347	The plague sweeps through Europe.
The Black Death strikes Norway.	1349		
The Kalmar Union is formed between Norway, Denmark, and Sweden.	1397	1453	Ottoman Turks capture Constantinople, conquering the Byzantine Empire.
		1492	Columbus arrives in North America.
Sweden leaves the Kalmar Union.	1523	1500s	Reformers break away from the Catholic Church, and Protestantism is born.
Denmark-Norway officially converts from Catholic to Lutheran.	1536	1776	The U.S. Declaration of Independence is signed.
		1789	The French Revolution begins.

NORWEGIAN HISTORY

Following the Napoleonic Wars, Norway is joined with Sweden.	**Early 1800s**
Norway grants all men the right to vote.	**1898**
Norway ends its union with Sweden, becoming fully independent.	**1905**
Norwegian Roald Amundsen leads the first party to reach the South Pole.	**1911**
Great Britain uses Norway's merchant fleet during World War I, and many of the ships are destroyed.	**1914–1918**
German forces invade Norway and occupy it for the rest of World War II.	**1940**
Oil is discovered in Norwegian territory under the North Sea.	**1968**
Gro Harlem Brundtland becomes Norway's first female prime minister.	**1981**
Conservative Party leader Erna Solberg becomes prime minister.	**2013**

WORLD HISTORY

1865	The American Civil War ends.
1879	The first practical lightbulb is invented.
1914	World War I begins.
1917	The Bolshevik Revolution brings communism to Russia.
1929	A worldwide economic depression begins.
1939	World War II begins.
1945	World War II ends.
1969	Humans land on the Moon.
1975	The Vietnam War ends.
1989	The Berlin Wall is torn down as communism crumbles in Eastern Europe.
1991	The Soviet Union breaks into separate states.
2001	Terrorists attack the World Trade Center in New York City and the Pentagon near Washington, D.C.
2004	A tsunami in the Indian Ocean destroys coastlines in Africa, India, and Southeast Asia.
2008	The United States elects its first African American president.

Fast Facts

Name of country: Norway

Year of independence: 1905

National anthem: No official anthem, but "Ja, Vi Elsker Dette Landet" ("Yes, We Love This Country") is often used

Official language: Norwegian

Bergen

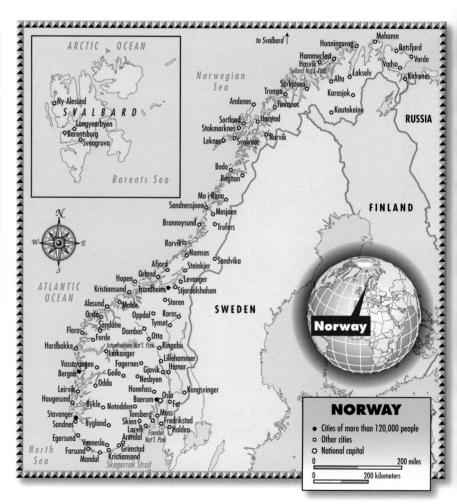

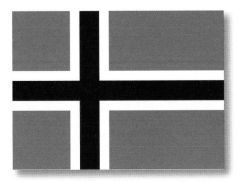

National flag

Geirangerfjord

Official religion:	None
Type of government:	Constitutional monarchy
Head of state:	King
Head of government:	Prime minister
Area:	125,021 square miles (323,802 sq km)
Bordering countries:	Sweden to the east; Finland and Russia to the northeast
Highest elevation:	Galdhopiggen, 8,100 feet (2,469 m) above sea level
Lowest elevation:	Sea level along the coast
Longest river:	Glomma River, 372 miles (599 km) long
Largest lake:	Mjosa, 142 square miles (368 sq km)
Longest fjord:	Sognefjord, 127 miles (204 km)
Warmest month:	July, with an average daytime temperature of 71°F (22°C)
Coolest month:	January, with an average daytime temperature of 31°F (−0.5°C)
Highest recorded temperature:	96.1°F (35.6°C) in Nesbyen, Buskerud, June 1970
Lowest recorded temperature:	−60.5°F (−51.4°C) in Karasjok, Finnmark, January 1886
Average annual precipitation:	In Oslo, 30 inches (76 cm)

Stavanger

Currency

National population (2016 est.):	5,265,158	
Population of major cities (2016 est.):	Oslo	660,987
	Bergen	278,120
	Trondheim	187,951
	Stavanger	132,895
	Baerum	122,660

Landmarks:
- ▶ *Geirangerfjord,* Sunnmore
- ▶ *Jotunheimen National Park,* Oppland
- ▶ *National Museum of Art, Architecture, and Design,* Oslo
- ▶ *Nidaros Cathedral,* Trondheim
- ▶ *Viking Ship Museum,* Oslo

Economy: Norway controls large oil reserves under the North Sea. It is the largest oil producer of any European nation. It is also a major producer of natural gas. Shipping and shipbuilding are both major industries. Foods, paper products, metals, textiles, and chemicals are all produced in Norway. Sheep, cattle, and pigs are valuable livestock raised in Norway. Norwegian farmers also grow barley, potatoes, wheat, and carrots. Some fishers head out to sea to gather their catch, while others raise fish on fish farms.

Currency: In 2016, 1 krone equaled 12 U.S. cents, and US$1.00 equaled 8.33 kroner.

System of weights and measures: Metric system

Literacy rate: 100%

Schoolchildren

Gro Harlem Brundtland

Norwegian words and phrases:

Ja	Yes
Nei	No
Vaer sa snill	Please
Takk	Thank you
Vaer sa god	You're welcome
Unnskyld	Excuse me
Beklager	I am sorry
God morgen	Good morning
God kveld	Good evening
God natt	Good night

Prominent Norwegians:

Roald Amundsen (1872–1928)
Antarctic explorer

Gro Harlem Brundtland (1939–)
Prime minister

Magnus Carlsen (1990–)
Chess champion

Kirsten Flagstad (1895–1962)
Opera singer

Thor Heyerdahl (1914–2002)
Explorer and anthropologist

Edvard Munch (1863–1944)
Painter

Sigrid Undset (1882–1949)
Novelist

To Find Out More

Books

- Asbjornsen, Peter Christen, and Jorgen Moe. *Norwegian Folktales*. Amazon Digital Services, 2012.

- Klingel, Cynthia. *Leif Eriksson: Norwegian Explorer*. North Mankato, MN: Children's World, 2014.

- Undset, Sigrid. *Happy Times in Norway*. Minneapolis: University of Minnesota Press, 2013.

Music

- Grieg, Edvard. *The Best of Grieg Including the Piano Concerto in A Minor*. Philips, 1993.

- *Song of Norway*. London: Stage Door Records, 2013.

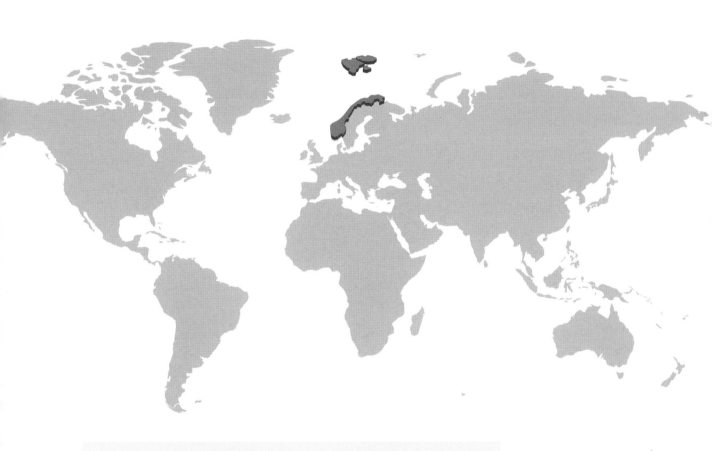

▶ Visit this Scholastic Web site for more information on Norway:
www.factsfornow.scholastic.com
Enter the keyword **Norway**

Index

Page numbers in *italics*
indicate illustrations.

desserts, 123–124
fish, 122
julekake, 124
kringla, 125, *125*
krumkake, 123–124, *124*
meats, 121–122, *122*
recipe, 125, *125*
side-dishes, 123
whale meat, 34
Fredrikstad, 21
funerals, 121

G

Galdhopiggen, 16, 20
games, 127
Geirangerfjord, *18*, 19
geography
    coastline, 18, 22
    elevation, 16, 20
    fjords, 11, *11*, 16, 18–19, *18*
    islands, 17, 22, *22*, 24
    lakes, 16, *19*, 21
    land area, 15, 16
    mountains, 19–20, *19*, *20*, *22*
    plateaus, 21
    rivers, 16, 21
    tundra, *21*
Germany, 54–55, *55*, 75
glaciers, 39, 41
Glomma River, 16, 21
government
    Christian People's Party, 65
    coalitions, 64–65
    Coastal Party, 65
    Conservative Party, 53, *64*, 65
    constitution, 59, 95
    Council of State, 61
    early settlers, 43
    elections, 59, 63–64
    European Union (EU), 70

executive branch, 59–61, 66, 133, *133*
independence, 53–54, 85
judicial branch, 65
Kalmar Union, 49, *49*
Labor Party, 57, 65
languages and, 85
legislative branch, 53–54, 58, 63–65, *63*, 66
Liberal Party, 53, 65
ministries, 61
national parks and, 39
oil industry and, 12
parliamentary parties, 65
prime ministers, 61, *64*, 133, *133*
Progress Party, 65
religion and, 95
Sami Parliament of Norway, 81
Sami people and, 65, 80–81
Sami People's Party, 65
social services, 12, 56, 69, 76, 117, 118–119, 120
Storting, 63–65, *63*
term limits, 63
whaling industry and, 34
grass snakes, 30–31, *30*
Great Britain, 50, 54, 55
Greenland, 45, 92
Grieg, Edvard, 108
Gronland neighborhood, 83
Growth of the Soil (Knut Hamsun), 105
Gulf Stream, 24–25

H

Haakon the Good, 101
Hamsun, Knut, 105
Haraldsen, Sonja, 61, *61*
Harald V (king), *60*, 61, *61*, 81
Hardanger Plateau, 21
Headhunters (film), 110

health care, 12, 56, 76, *76*, 77, 120
Hedda Gabler (Henrik Ibsen), 104–105
Heyerdahl, Thor, 27, *27*, 133
Hinnoya Island, 22
historical maps. *See also* maps.
    Kalmar Union, *49*
    Viking Expansion, *45*
Historical Museum, 67
Hitler, Adolf, 54–55
holidays, 124, 125, 127
Holmenkollen Ski Museum, 113
housing, 13, 23, 43, 126
humpback whales, *33*
hunter-gatherers, 41

I

Ibsen, Henrik, 103, *103*, 104
Ibsen, Tancred, 109, *109*
Iceland, 34, 45, 92
Icelandic language, 82, 83
immigration
    economy and, 57
    Oslo, 67, 82, *82*, 83
    population of, 81–82, *82*
    religion and, 96, 97
independence, 53–54, 85
Islamic religion, 83, 86, 96, 97
islands
    Hinnoya, 22
    Lofoten Islands, 22, *22*, *116*
    Senja, 22
    Svalbard Islands, 17, 22, 24, 32, *84*
    Vesteralen Islands, 33

J

"Ja, Vi Elsker Dette Landet" (national anthem), 62
jazz music, *108*
Jotunheimen National Park, 39
Judaism, 86, 98

judicial branch of government, 65

julekake (dessert), 124

K

Kalmar Union, 49, *49*

Karpov, Anatoly, 115

Kasparov, Garry, 115

king eider ducks, *36*

Knausgaard, Karl Ove, 106

Kola Peninsula settlement, 51

Kon-Tiki Expedition by Raft Across the South Seas, The (Thor Heyerdahl), 27

kringla (cookies), 125, *125*

Kristin Lavransdatter (Sigrid Undset), *105*

krone (currency), 75, *75*

krumkake (dessert), 123–124, *124*

L

Labor Party, 57, 64, 65

Lake Mjosa, 16, 21

Lake Ringedalsvatnet, *19*

languages. *See also* people.

    Bokmal, 84, 85

    Corded Ware culture, 42

    dialects, 83–84

    Norwegian, 82–85, *84*

    Nynorsk, 84, 85, 104, *104*

    runic alphabet, *100*, 101

    Sami people, 80

Larvik, 27

leatherback sea turtles, 30, 31, *31*

legislative branch of government, 53–54, 58, 63–65, *63*, 66

leisure time, 126–127, *126*, *127*

Liberal Party, 53, 65

life expectancy, *56*, 120

literature, 27, 101–106, *103*, 133

livestock, 42, *71*, 72, 107

Lofoten Islands, 22, *22*, 116

longships, *43*, 44

Longyearbyen, 17

lower secondary school, 87

lumber industry, 49, 77

Luster, 88

Lutheranism, 94–95, *95*

Luther, Martin, 94

Lysefjord, *11*

M

manufacturing, 52, 55, 71, 74, 77, 118

maps. *See also* historical maps.

    geopolitical, *10*

    Oslo, 67

    population density, 80

    resources, *74*

    topographical, 16

    traditional Sami lands, *81*

marathon running, 115

Margaret I, queen of Denmark, *48*, 49

marine life

    Atlantic salmon, 35, *35*

    cod, 22, 34

    fishing, 34, 126

    fishing industry, 22, 73, *73*, 74

    salmon, 35, *35*, 73, 122, *123*

    whales, 32–33, *33*, 34, *34*

marine parks, 39

marriage, 121, *121*

Max Manus (film), 110, *110*

Meltzer, Fredrik, 60

merchant ships, 54

Middle Ages, 105, *105*

mining, 49, 71, 74, 77

minke whales, 34

Miss Tati, *108*

monarchs

    Erik VII, 49

    Harald V, 60, 61, *61*, 81

    Margaret I, *48*, 49

    Olaf I, 92–93

Olaf II, 46, *46*, 93, *93*

mosques, 97, *97*

Munch, Edvard, 112, *112*, 133

municipalities. *See also* counties.

    Luster, 88

    Nesbyen, 16

museums, 67

music, 62, 75, 106–108, *106*, *107*, 133

My Struggle (Karl Ove Knausgaard), 106

N

Napoleon, emperor of France, 50

Napoleonic Wars, 50

national anthem, 62

national bird, 37, *37*

national flag, 60, *60*

national holidays, 127

National Museum of Art, Architecture, and Design, 67

national parks, 39, *39*

National Theatre, 67, *67*

natural gas, 69, 70, 74, 77

Nazi Party, 54–55, *55*, 110, *110*

Nidaros Cathedral, 23, 94, *94*

Nidelva River, 23

nighttime, 17

Nine Homeworlds, 92, *92*

Ninety-five Theses, 94

Nobel Prize, 105

Nordraak, Rikard, 62

northern lights, 25, *25*

North Sea, 15, 68, *68*, 69, 70

Norwegian Folk Museum, 67

Norwegian language, 82–85

Norwegian Sea, 15

Norwegian University of Science and Technology, 87

Nynorsk language, 84, 85, 104, *104*

Meet the Author

WIL MARA IS THE AWARD-WINNING author of more than two hundred books, many of them educational titles for children published by Scholastic. He began writing in the late 1980s with several nonfiction titles about herpetology. He branched out into fiction in the mid-1990s, when he ghostwrote five of the popular Boxcar Children Mysteries. He has since authored more than a dozen novels, including *Wave*, which received the 2005 New Jersey Notable Book Award, *The Gemini Virus*, and the *New York Times* bestseller *Frame 232*, which reached the number-one spot in its category on Amazon.com and won the 2013 Lime Award for Excellence in Fiction.

Photo Credits